OUT
OF THE
PIT

HANNAH PARKISON

ISBN 978-1-64299-392-9 (paperback)
ISBN 978-1-64299-393-6 (digital)

Christian Faith Publishing, Inc.
832 Park Avenue
Meadville, PA 16335
www.christianfaithpublishing.com

Printed in the United States of America

CONTENTS

OUT OF THE PIT

He lifted me out of the pit of despair, out of mud and the mire. He set my feet on solid ground and steadied me as I walked.

—Psalm 40:2

How does one start the beginning sentence of a book? Do I go the formal route with structure and no denying I have a college education, or the new hip way of just throwing it all out there and hoping for the best? Hi, I am new here, and I greatly appreciate you giving me, an unknown author to the world, a chance. Personally, some of the best books I have read were written by previously unknown authors who experienced a spiritual transformation with God-given strength. I believe God allows us to go through these difficult times to not only grow in our own faith but to be there for others when they experience similar circumstances. I was driving in my car one afternoon when the idea of writing this came to me. I was listening to a worship song and had such a burst of energy come out of nowhere. Ideas started flooding my mind, almost as if they had been stored and waiting to make their way through all along. Visions of scripture and my testimony intertwined in my head, and I honestly was caught off guard, but certain this was no mistake. The song ended and I pulled into the driveway to enter the house as reality smacked me in the face. I opened the door to pure chaos as my five-year-old was begging for dinner, and the baby was stumbling as he tried to get his footing as a new walker.

Being an anxious thinker, thoughts came to my mind, like "Nice dream, but you're a mom with young, busy kids—and you have a bachelor's in business, by the way." I literally believed every lie that approached me, especially that I was not fit for this task. I would even get discouraged after reading about the authors of my devotionals, all stating they had theology degrees next to their names. Each time I read them, I felt unqualified for my vision just because I didn't feel equipped.

What makes someone qualified to share their testimony and lead others anyway? I had recently read the top 5 reasons couples do not make it in their marriage were infidelity, military, loss of child, finances, and moving. I am happy to say we have never had an issue with infidelity, but we have been through four of the five. Now, going through these very hard things that I know God allowed me to go through for a reason, do you think He would say, "You are not qualified until you get a proper education?" I am not saying people waste their time going to school to be teachers of God's word, we need them desperately. I believe God can speak through anyone with any background, and if you don't understand that your sole identity is "Child of God," Satan will have no problem assigning you a new one. So here I am, just a wife and a mom, with a testimony I'd love to share in hopes of helping others.

I am not sure what condition you are in, but I have been in the pit. Not just a pit, *the* pit. Since God pulled me through, I have had a strong passion to be there for anyone that is hurting and possibly in that place too. God started bringing people into my life that were going through some very dark times, and I realized the gift of compassion and empathy I possessed. I strongly believe God brings people into our lives that have the ability to empathize with us, and it gives us earthly comfort. I have seen the result of helping others, so I wanted to personally bring it to a larger scale and write this book.

I am prayerfully going to try my best to format this as if I were coaching myself back when I had depression. I know the triggers and what to avoid talking about in order to not worsen the situation. I will do my best to be sensitive but also real about what you are going through. I have full confidence in God to help me guide you out of your pit. Before I begin, I would like to pray for you as you enter this journey:

"Dear God, you know this child of yours by name, you knit them together in their own mother's womb. You know every single ounce of their trials and pain, and they desperately need you maybe more than they know right now. Please guide me in the best way to help shine a light on their situation and show them you. I thank you for never leaving or forsaking us and loving us through it all. Please bring healing to this child and remind them during difficult times that they are more than conquerors! We love you God. In Jesus's name, I pray, amen."

MY TESTIMONY

I grew up in a very loving and God-fearing home with a mother, father, and younger sister. We went to a nondenominational Christian church every Sunday, and my parents were heavily involved in various ministries. Every year we were taken to Walt Disney World, and we have more home videos than anyone I know. My home was completely full of love and nurturing in all ways possible. I am by no means trying to brag about my upbringing, but I am simply trying to convey that anyone can develop anxiety and depression, even if their life wasn't difficult prior. If my childhood was so smooth-sailing, then what in the world did I need to be anxious or depressed over?

My family had planned a small summer vacation to Cedar Point and Sea World in Ohio. We had some road trip hours ahead of us so we grabbed some breakfast from a fast-food restaurant and eventually reached the park. We went on with our day, rode roller coasters, begged to play rigged, cheap prize-winning games, etc. A couple hours in, we find ourselves at an IMAX theater watching a film on life in the ocean. All of a sudden, my younger sister gets out of her seat and starts running to the exit. On the way there, she had gotten sick and left a trail of yuck all the way down the aisle. It was very traumatic for her as she was crying and embarrassed in front of a theater full of people. My parents figured that it was probably the breakfast sandwich we had eaten that morning since she had only gotten sick once. Within seconds of that conclusion leaving my parent's mouths, I developed symptoms of sweat, nausea, racing heart, panic, fogginess, etc. My official what-if thinking had established its first imprint on my mind. "What if I throw up in front of everyone and cry? I did eat that same sandwich. It is only a matter of time until my life is ruined as well." Once I had come up with enough evidence to support my what-ifs, they turned into "When will this happen?" And there you have it: a panic attack at the age of nine. I will tell you this though: *it never happened.* I was certain of becoming a victim, so I held a bag up to my face the entire time. Since my sister seemed to be on the mend, my parents decided to stay another day and try to enjoy the trip. I even talked my parents into getting me a stroller because I was so convinced I was sick. There I was, sure of my upcoming sickness, and I am far away from home in an obnoxious amusement park full of large crowds and noise. Quite a perfect setting for an anxious mind, but I made it out of there alive.

Fall had come and it was time for school again, and my obsessive thinking carried itself into my life as a fourth grader. I still was very anxious of throwing up and would call home sick from school constantly because of this fear. I remember getting the same symptoms I had developed during my first panic attack, and I made myself believe I was truly ill. This scenario would repeat itself over and over in many other situations as a young child. I avoided so many fun activities and birthday parties because of my plagued present moment. I learned to just accept my anxious mind as something I would just have to deal with forever. It was my mental bully, and I allowed it to beat me to a pulp. I felt so differently than others and determined that something was just plain wrong with me.

Out of innocent obligation, I was baptized at the age of nine—I really wanted to partake in communion and be "mature." I meant well and I believed in God, but there is so much more that I didn't understand at the time. I would have gone to heaven by accepting Jesus into my heart and naming Him my Savior, but I didn't have a daily personal relationship with Him. I knew the stories, and the beliefs of my faith, but I so badly wanted that genuine ache that people had for God in their lives. I felt that if I tried to display that, it wouldn't be genuine. I would look around during worship at church and see people literally crying out to Him while their hands were raised in the air, like they just wanted God to pick them up. These people expressed such a personal desperation for God that it visually seemed their life depended on it. How could I obtain that—was it just not meant for me?

Looking back, I understand now why I didn't feel this way naturally, I thought I had all that my flesh needed and was in no need of immediate rescue. I coasted this way all the way to college until my aunt (with whom I was very close) took her own life. I think I was shocked more than anything, but I managed to continue school and work, and push on for about a year while trying to process what happened. Sure, I was completely sad and had nightmares of what occurred, but I didn't handle it properly. I didn't go to God, not once.

At the exact one-year anniversary of her death, my whole world changed drastically. This perfect storm was buried deep within me without my knowledge. During college, I was a nanny and watched kids from multiple families. It was 2008. I was in my junior year, and I was babysitting after a long day of school. I had just put the kids to bed after a fun night of playing and I grabbed some coffee. I sat down on the couch to relax, but all of a sudden, I started to panic out of nowhere. I felt like I needed to run. To this day, I do not know the trigger for this particular attack, but it hit me like a ton of bricks. Within seconds, my hope in general was completely gone, and I started questioning who I was and where I was going in life. I developed all the common symptoms of a panic attack and newborn fear was ever so present. This "dark cloud" formed above me, and no matter where I would go, it would follow. I would get up and walk around their house hoping that scenery change was all I needed, but the feeling remained heavily. I was so scared, but I didn't even know why.

To most outsiders, my life was going amazingly well. I had a job, an education in the works, and a loving family. I called my mom right away with confidence she would make this foreign feeling disappear. I remember the conversation so well: "Mom, I am freaking out. I am very anxious for no reason and I have no hope. I am scared and I don't understand what is going on." She was confused and reminded me it had been a long day and told me to stop by after work. Now I am being fully honest with you. I believed my mom could single-handedly fix this, since she had fixed everything else in my life thus far. It is natural for a child to run into the arms of their mother or father in times of hardship. When my children fall and bump their head, they will immediately scan the room for my husband or me with their arms raised. Usually there will be lots of tears, but as soon as they are soothed and told it will be okay, they calm down and are able to pick up where they left off.

At the time, I was living in my own apartment about thirty minutes from home and decided to stay the night at my parents' because of how unstable I felt. I figured I just needed some rest and an encouraging chat with my mom and dad. I was so scared that I actually made my mom sleep on my floor. I didn't know it at the time, but I was trying to fight a spiritual battle in my mind with my mom as my weapon. Sitting here visualizing it makes me giggle, but it is true. I can just picture my mom shrinking and stepping into my mind and fighting "bad guys." It became apparent to me though that my mom couldn't fix this. It wasn't something tangible for her to battle. I remember waking up the next day and still feeling this anxiety-driven hopelessness.

My father had experienced anxiety and depression, and because of his history, he was able to relate to this new scary feeling and offer advice. I went in to work the next day at my nanny job and I remember taking the kids to the mall play place while my head was swimming in this storm. I still could not shake this feeling, and I started second-guessing myself as a caretaker for children in this state of mind. I decided to go to my primary care doctor to get some blood work done and talk about possible medication. The doctor checked my vitals, asked what my symptoms were, and made certain I was not considering suicide (which really set off my obsessive thinking!). I had my blood drawn and was hoping that something was just off, and I was deficient in some type of vitamin that could be fixed with a supplement. To my disappointment, my numbers were great and did not reflect this overpowering emptiness inside of me. I wanted a reason for this feeling, something to point my finger at, something to blame. I ended up going on a low dose of an antidepressant and an anti-anxiety medication for panic attacks. Part of me knew that this wasn't going to solely fix my problem, something was wrong with me, and I was lost in a maze of confusion.

I started focusing on things I did not currently have at this point in my life. I did not have a steady boyfriend, which led to the thought of never getting married or having children. I had completely lost my confidence in myself, and my mind just continued to wander. My what-if thinking had returned at full force and just snowballed into a big mess. I ended up having to quit my job as a nanny and temporarily moved in with my parents. Ironically the week after my depression hit hard, we had a Disney trip planned. I was confident that it would be enough of a distraction to dissolve my depression. We arrived in Orlando with Mickey and bright-colored signs in our face, and I literally felt nothing. One day we were at the resort pool and I recall thinking, "Do I even care to swim anymore?" I had completely lost my joy and was just going through the motions while watching everyone else love life. I literally had no motivation to do the things I once loved. During the trip, my father helped guide me out of my what-if thinking constantly and reminded me that this feeling was going to get better as I progressed on the medication. I really wanted to believe him, but there was a so much doubt in me. My mind was on a rollercoaster full of ups and downs with no end in sight. Every day commitments were daunting and felt ten times harder to accomplish.

I started opening up to friends about my anxiety and depression and that is when I allowed God to make his entrance into my situation. Again, I believed in Him and knew He could do great things, but I felt far too gone and unworthy. I was not hopeful in the fact that God come to my rescue. I became stripped of all forms of earthly comforts, and that is where He wanted me. God should have been the first place to run to, but I left Him as a last resort. Friends started sending me Bible verses, worship songs, encouraging thoughts, and I became desperate for God. Remember my longing to have that very emotional interaction with God during worship that I saw in everyone else? Oh, how I gained that desire effortlessly as a natural spiritual need! All these worship songs mimicked my current state, and I was whole heartedly meaning what was coming out of my mouth as

I cried out to God. This jump-started my brand-new walk with God, but it wasn't easy.

Now I don't know your exact situation, but I assume you are needing some guidance or you wouldn't be reading this book. How badly do you want victory over this? Aren't you tired of wasting your time in a pit of despair while watching others joyfully live life? Decide right now that you will not allow your joy to be stolen anymore and that you are willing to let God lead you out of this mess and enjoy your life! If you are willing, I have prayerfully developed an outlined plan to lead you through this valley with God by your side. I am ready when you are!

GETTING STARTED

Before we get too deep into this journey, I want to say that it is very important for you to get checked out by your doctor due to the symptoms you may be experiencing. Please take my advice without alarm and understand that while it may be hard to seek medical advice when you already have so much anxiety, it is important. I am sure your what-if radar is blaring with just the thought of going to get examined—I know mine was. Sometimes there is a medical cause for the way you are feeling that can be altered by supplements or medication. I try to view this as a simple bridge to travel on toward healing. There can be a chemical imbalance within the brain and an antidepressant or supplement under a medical doctor's watchful eye may be helpful. I myself did go on a mild antidepressant short term that aided me in my breakthrough. Like I mentioned in my testimony, a drug will not solely fix you unfortunately but can be helpful if there is a medical explanation for needing one. If it is recommended by your doctor to take a medication and you are struggling with what to do, pray and ask God for guidance.

Now, I want to take a quick glance at your faith. Without your faith in God, this plan for attacking anxiety and depression will be ineffective. I was blessed to be raised in a home where I was taught about God on a consistent basis. I understand this is not the case for many, but wherever you are in your walk with God, please know that you are His child and He loves you so. John 3:16 says, "For God so loved the world that he gave his one and only Son, that whoever believes in him shall not perish but have eternal life."

God is our Heavenly Father and not only loves us more than we can fathom, but his heart aches for us in our suffering. You did not stumble upon this or other sources pointing you to Him because of luck. It is in alignment with His plan for you. Jeremiah 29:11 says, "'For I know the plans I have for you,' declares the Lord, 'plans to prosper you and not harm you, plans to give you hope and a future.'"

Speaking of plans, yours was specifically hand-crafted by God before you were ever born into this world: "For you created my inmost being; you knit me together in my mother's womb" (Ps. 139:13).

I decided to write this book for anyone at any level of faith. I entered my journey of depression and anxiety with a good amount of knowledge on God but had a near nonexistent relationship with Him. You may be on the verge of taking that leap to follow God in your life wondering if this may be too overwhelming for you. My full intentions are to simplify and break down what is emotionally, physically, mentally, and spiritually going on during your struggle. Therefore, all are welcome! I do not know your background or how you eventually got to this place of shear desperation, but there are many tools Satan will use to contribute to getting you there. There will be many "traps" on your journey set up specifically by the enemy himself to tempt you to quit. In fact, once you decided to face anxiety and depression with defeat in mind, he already began coordinating a plan against it.

Check out this good example of this type of opposition: My cousin and her family decided to find a church where they could learn and grow in the Lord. They had only been once to a particular church, but they knew it was where they belonged right away. She gave me all the details in a very excited tone and had an immediate new outlook on life. It was like a child describing their Christmas morning. Later in the evening, she had gotten a phone call with some very upsetting news. I was trying my best to console her (keep in mind this was a Saturday night and the next day was Sunday). It was evident that this was enough of a distraction for her to most likely dismiss the need to go to church the next day. It took me a minute to understand this developing spiritual battle right before my eyes, but I am so glad I caught it. She was reaching a huge level in her faith and Satan didn't like that. I ended up interrupting her tears to tell her what was going on here as her eyes widened while processing it all. She calmed down and continued to analyze the problem the rest of the night. The very next day, she called me to tell me they did end up going to church, and it had been an amazing service she couldn't imagine missing! God pulled her through and she ignored Satan's attack. Oh, how badly Satan wanted her to dwell at home in this upsetting news and regress in her walk with God.

YOU ARE WORTH IT

I have heard many excuses (and have given them myself) when it comes to fighting this tiresome battle. Shame was ever so present in my life as I felt like I was such a waste of time for my family and God. Not only was I pushing myself further into a pit, but I was also worried I was pushing my family away by becoming so desperate and needy. Take a deep breath of relief because coming from someone on the other side, you are worth it. The Bible states this confirmation many, many times! A parable I always come back to when struggling with worth is one Jesus was teaching his disciples in Luke 15:4:"Suppose one of you has a hundred sheep and loses one of them. Doesn't he leave the ninety-nine in the open country and go after the lost sheep until he finds it?"

This is reflective of our relationship with God in the fact that He is our shepherd and we are His sheep. He is saying that when we go "astray" (in any way, shape, or form), it is still worth it to Him to search for and rescue us every single time! Meaning everyone here on earth holds the same value in God's eyes, and you are of enough worth to Him because He loves you unconditionally. There is not one situation that God cannot pull you out of, and there is no such thing as "too far gone" in God's eyes.

> "But He has said to me, 'My grace is sufficient for you [My loving kindness and My mercy are more than enough—always available—*regardless of the situation*]'" (2 Cor. 12:9).

Let me introduce you to a man in the Bible named Job. Now I am not going to even try to play the comparison game, but this guy had it bad. Unimaginably bad. Any time I am going through something difficult, I will remind myself, "At least I am not Job." Check out Job 1:13–19:

> One day when Job's sons and daughters were feasting and drinking wine at the oldest brother's house, a messenger came to Job and said, "The oxen were plowing and the donkeys were grazing nearby, and the Sabeans attacked and made off with them. They put the servants to the sword, and I am the only one who has escaped to tell you!" While he was still speaking, another messenger came and said, "The fire of God fell from the Heavens and burned up the sheep and the servants, and I am the only one who has escaped to tell you!" While he was still speaking, another messenger came and said, "The Chaldeans formed three raiding parties and swept down on your camels and made off with them. They put the servants to the sword, and I am the only one who has escaped to tell you!" While he was still speaking, yet another messenger came and said, "Your sons and daughters were feasting and drinking wine at the oldest brother's house, when suddenly a mighty wind swept in from the desert and struck the four corners of the house. It collapsed on them and they are dead, and I am the only one who has escaped to tell you!"

Oh, but wait, there is added turmoil in Job 2:7: "So Satan went out from the presence of the Lord and afflicted Job with painful sores from the soles of his feet to crown his head. Then Job took a piece of broken pottery and scraped himself with it and sat among the ashes.

His wife said to him "Are you still maintaining your integrity? Curse God and die!"

My man Job, bless his heart. He endured a lot physically, spiritually, mentally, and emotionally. He stayed faithful to God and did not curse Him despite his dreadful circumstances and outside influences. He was rewarded heavily after his breakthrough for his faith as he gained double what he had previously had:

> After Job had prayed for his friends, the Lord restored his fortunes and gave him twice as much as he had before...The Lord blessed the latter part of Job's life more than the former part. He had fourteen thousand sheep, six thousand camels, a thousand yoke of oxen and a thousand donkeys. And he also had seven sons and three daughters...After this, Job lived a hundred and forty years; he saw his children and their children to the fourth generation. And so Job died, an old man and full of years.(Job 42:10, 2–13, 16–17)

Good things will come out of this, believe it or not! If you need a reminder, go back and read Job until you realize if he can make it, so can you! Halfway into his story, it's pretty understandable to think that there is no way this could end well, but God made it happen.

Speaking of good things, the third page in my journal (which was dated only twenty-five days after my onset of anxiety and depression) has a list of things that were already proving themselves to be true:

- Closer to God in trust and my purpose
- Bonding with family
- Strength
- Love myself
- Get rid of bad habits
- Take the time to visit people and relax
- Reach out to those suffering as well

- Depend fully on God
- Learn more about God
- Desire to seek God
- How to deal with negative thoughts
- Can't love anything more than God
- Objects mean nothing compared to God
- Can't get stressed as easily

These are all things that were missing prior to my depression, and I am so grateful that I gained them, even though this was a difficult time. You can too! Make a list of goals you want to reach—borrow from my example if you wish. I also made a list of things I desired for my future, because at this point, I found hope in my future! With this new godly outlook on life, things had shifted a bit, and I needed something to look forward to. When we are depressed, it's so easy to forget the things that bring us joy, since we are so centered on ourselves and our condition. These goals were written down in checklist form, and I went back recently and checked them all off. Oh, how God provided!

- Love God
- Husband
- Three to four kids
- Live somewhere warm
- Have a dog
- Be a full-time mom
- Go to Disney World
- Have a home church
- Be a great mom
- Have a nice house
- Great in-laws
- Be a great cook
- Be adventurous
- Close with family
- Have a mini van
- Garden

- Have nice neighbors
- Have fun toys for the kids
- Eat healthily
- Have barbecues with friends and family

This is my life currently and then some. I am by no means bragging about it, but it shows the provision that came from God alone. I wrote this literally a year before dating my husband, and I remember thinking, "Well, even if I get a few of these, it would be awesome." Don't get me wrong, I battled thoughts over this list. There was such a loud and persistent force denying these dreams during my entire journey. But I pursued God and followed His lead, and I am continuously blessed after my breakthrough. God has given me more than I deserve. There is light at the end of the tunnel, I promise. You just have to persevere:

> "You need to persevere so that when you have done the will of God, you will receive what he has promised" (Heb. 10:36).

WHAT EXACTLY IS GOING ON HERE?

When I was going through my anxiety and depression, I felt like I personally was going crazy. Everyone was trying their best to reassure me that this was a false assumption, but I didn't believe them. Everyone gets to this level of despair under different circumstances, and not one story is the same. I think for my situation I didn't want to face the terrible negative influences on my mind, but it is the first step toward healing. These influences are ugly and usually slip by without being caught, leaving you to think something is just plain *wrong with you*. Rest assured, nothing is wrong with you and people struggle with this more than you know! I didn't want to believe I had a problem with the condition of my mind because it made me feel weak. There is a stigma involved when it comes to anxiety and depression, and people allow themselves to be labeled by their condition.

These negative influences are to blame and may seem like common sense to you, but all are huge pushy, dangerous, deteriorating influences on your mind. In order to understand the intensity of the impact, let's take a good look at the mind first.

THE MIND

You do not have to be a scientist to realize how powerful, amazing, intricate, and fragile the mind can be. Let's take for an example the current state you are in. Outside influences aside, what you are going through mentally is based upon the functionality of the mind. Now I have said before, in certain doctor observed cases, I highly believe in a chemical imbalance needing to be aided with medication; however, we do have a big responsibility on our end. Sometimes our circumstances are out of our control, but the way we mentally, emotionally, and spiritually handle them will determine our breakthrough. During my first panic attack, it is evident that my mind was so capable of having power over the entire situation that it caused actual physical symptoms. All it took was a simple "what if" and suddenly I have sweat, racing heart, confusion, nausea, etc. The mind is so underestimated that these symptoms are thought to be occurring naturally, proving our fears to be real. Your mind is giving its best shot to detour you from what is really bothering you. Once your fear originates, your mind is totally on overload, and it disperses these thoughts into "symptoms." My mind wanted me to take the focus off the fear itself and think about these new crazy symptoms I was having. We then form a repetitious habit of this, causing obsessive thoughts for our fears to build on, making it extremely difficult to break free.

FEAR

I remember my mom constantly reminding me during my dark times, "This all started with a fear." While this annoyed me at the time because of its simplicity, she was right. You would not be in the position you are in if it weren't for fear. Webster's Dictionary defines *fear* as "the emotion experienced in presence or threat of danger," or "An uneasy state of mind usually over the possibility of an anticipated misfortune or trouble." Everyone experiences fear at certain intensities in their lifetime and handle it differently. Random thoughts of fear would be introduced, and they would paralyze my mind. My present moment was completely robbed by this crippling new fear, and I was analyzing and dissecting to make sense of it. This is the core of my first panic attack at the amusement park, the fear of throwing up and being embarrassed. There of course are common fears like flying, heights, bridges, etc. Everyone tends to make light of these with a nervous giggle, while they avoid them at all costs. It's easy—you avoid planes, rock climbing, and bridges, but what about the fears that plague your mind because you have no control over avoiding them?

When my depression first made its ugly appearance, I had many new fears of things physically out of my control. I was afraid of never being in love, never having children, and never getting out of this dark, empty, and scary feeling. These weren't tangible things I could avoid. They were simply scary thoughts of my unknown future. These scary thoughts seemed to reproduce in my mind, creating a snowball effect. Each thought would bring me to a new level of low and would make it that much harder to think my way out of. I would create a subconscious scary thought rotation that would mentally cripple me. I started to think I was going crazy, which created the fear of never returning back to my old self. Honestly, I created a scenario in my head of being thrown into a mental institution and never getting out. Now, this thought makes me laugh, but at the time, it felt like a real possibility. I had many people promising I would recover, but it wasn't enough for me. How did they know? I came to the point of understanding that no human on earth could fix this. It was up to me to figure it out.

When a fear is born within your mind, it is a form of entrapment, and it cannot physically be moved. Up until this point, I had cures for anything that brought me discomfort, but this caught me off guard. You can't "run away" from your mind—it follows you wherever you go! There is nowhere to hide from yourself as silly as that sounds. Walt Disney World is known to be the "Happiest Place on Earth," and even that didn't take my mind off how terrible I felt, my mind accompanied me on every ride. It actually made me feel worse in the sense that everyone was running around laughing having fun while I wallowed in this "jail" of my own mind.

ANXIETY

At this point, you are so accustomed to searching for fear that it becomes a job your mind has created for itself. Once you have been through a good amount of these fears and realize they aren't going away, you will develop your anxiety. Anxiety is a constant feeling of losing control or something bad happening. Fear honks its horn, your adrenaline takes flight and pushes you to move as your mind is saying, "Danger, danger!" You become anxious on a daily basis and have created a new unfortunate norm for yourself. With a simple unwanted thought, my mind talked itself into sheer panic from anxiety of the fear itself, eventually leading me into depression. Do you see how these all play their own role and transition straight into each other? This is a formation that lines up so perfectly that it causes us to question ourselves because the blueprint is well hidden. We start to solely concentrate on how we are feeling that we lose sight of the fact that we have our guard down.

Like I said earlier about the mind, it is on a mission to distract you from the original fear. Now, in order for complete distraction, these scary thoughts have to be good enough to overpower the original fear, hence why they are called "scary thoughts." Mine ranged from simple anxiety about embarrassing myself to "what if I get so bad that I harm myself?" I knew deep down inside that I would never do that, but the thought of it scared me into a fetal position. You will notice your new scary thoughts may have never concerned you before, and this is perfect evidence that they are just thoughts that you can eventually overcome. These attacks sometimes land people in the hospital because they honestly think something is malfunctioning in their body. It creates a viscous cycle of "what's wrong with me" which intensifies the body's reaction. This is especially frightening to people that have not grown up with an anxious mind. Most of the time, the doctor at the hospital will tell you that your vitals are fine while sending you on your way, and maybe referring you to a psychiatrist. First of all, having a hospital not be able to "fix" you, makes you feel like a goner. Secondly, the recommendation of a psychiatrist can turn anyone into thinking they are officially a goner. Remember, crazy people don't know they are crazy. I cannot tell you how many times I was told this.

OBSESSIVE THINKING

These fears become stuck and end up making an imprint on our mind creating an obsession that makes its rounds over and over for the duration of the day. Obsessive thinking makes it nearly impossible to not think about your fears. You gain tunnel vision and lose sight of your present moment unfortunately. Picture a carrousel gaining new passengers (fears) every couple of stops but no one gets off. This carrousel goes around and around at a very fast pace, and eventually the weight limit is exceeded and it breaks down. It's hard to keep up with these thoughts as they race through your mind and you start becoming frustrated because you can't just stop them. Sometimes you see right through these fears and think you're making progress, but they return full force the next day. I would even say them out loud to my parents in order to prove how stupid they sounded coming out of my own mouth. I needed verification and approval from an outsider that they were just plain silly. I remember going up to my father saying, "Dad, I need you to help me deflate a thought." I would hesitate to say it, but once I did, I realized that it was just an irrational thought. Now I am not saying that every thought is "stupid"—there are some validating thoughts out there. I am saying these out-of-nowhere, irrational thoughts are stupid because they aren't real.

I would wake up feeling better and would introduce the scary thought in my mind willingly to see if it still bothered me. I considered this practicing, but if I were a turtle, you would physically see me retracting back into my shell! It wouldn't bother me for a while during the day, but then would come the obsessing: "Am I sure it doesn't bother me? How about now?" I would repeat this all day, and then it would eventually bother me and I had myself to blame.

I have a five-year-old daughter, and we have come to the point where we sometimes cannot tell her something exciting until it's about to happen. Say we are going to have someone over during the weekend and its only Monday, she will ask if it is "time yet" until you are ready to hide from her somewhere in the house. I have tried distracting her but she will admit, "But, Mommy, I just can't stop thinking of it!" This is a positive obsession from excitement (not for Mommy) that isn't necessarily harmful, but it goes to show we naturally obsess.

I finally got to a point where instead of cowering to these fears, I got angry at them. I started seeing things I was missing and realizing I was allowing this to run its course on its own terms. My tunnel vision started cracking, and I could see the amazing world on the outside that I was not fully enjoying. A lot of people in depression feel weak and emotionless, leaving it very hard to become angry. I always tell people I'm coaching out of depression to work toward their "angry phase." This isn't anger that involves lashing out on others or yourself. This is a healthy anger toward what has tried to take over the reins of your mind—his name is Satan.

SATAN

A h, finally time to reveal the enemy behind your struggles and expose his sly tricks. He is depicted in our society as a little red man with horns and a pitchfork on your shoulder. Seems harmless, right? First Peter 5:8 (emphasis added) suggests otherwise:"Be self-controlled and alert. Your *enemy* the devil prowls around like a roaring lion looking for someone to devour."

Oh, how quickly our idea of him is altered after reading that verse! Satan makes his first noted move in the Bible with Adam and Eve (as a serpent). God had specifically commanded that fruit from the tree of the knowledge of good and evil not be eaten, but the serpent tempts Adam and Eve and succeeds at getting them to disobey God. Satan is a very patient being as he studies you enough to be sure of how to attack and make the biggest impact at the best time. Luke 4:1 says,

> "Jesus, full of the Holy Spirit, left the Jordan and was led by the Spirit into the wilderness, where for forty days he was tempted by the devil. He ate nothing during those days, and at the end of them he was hungry. The devil said to him, "If you are the son of God, tell this stone to become bread." Jesus answered, "It is written: Man shall not live on bread alone." The devil led him up to a high place and showed him in an instant all the kingdoms of the world. And he said to him, "I will give you all their authority and splendor; it has been given to me, and I can give it to any-

one I want to. If you worship, it will all be yours. Jesus answered, "It is written: 'Worship the Lord your God and serve him only." The devil led him to Jerusalem and had him stand on the highest point of the temple. "If you are the Son of God," he said, "throw yourself down from here. For it is written: "He will command his angels concerning you to guard you carefully; they will lift you up in their hands, so that you will not strike your foot against a stone." Jesus answered, "It is said 'Do not put the Lord your God to the test.'" *When the devil had finished all this tempting, he left him until an opportune time."*

Here, Satan was trying to talk Jesus into temptation, but since Jesus had told him to take a hike, he slithered away back to his drawing board. He could have kept on badgering Jesus right then and there, but he knew his plan was not working, "so he left him until an opportune time." I just picture a nasty villain in a movie that is constantly in some lab in a basement constructing these plans of attack. If Satan was bold enough to tempt the son of God, then he's bold enough to tempt you. His concentration is mainly on your mind, if he can slip through those cracks then we have a domino effect on the rest of your body. When we are in a state of depression, we no longer have the best self-care. We lose interest in physical activity, have symptoms of panic, loss of appetite, unhealthily increased appetite, and our physical appearance is not maintained. Before you know it, you have more health problems than what you started with just because of the condition of your mind, which makes your depression worsen.

We tend to grow weary in our heart as well and question whether God can really pull us out of this mess. Satan would love nothing more than for you to doubt the love and capability of God in your situation. We underestimate and sometimes even doubt God's mighty power in difficult times. Because Satan has studied you so closely, his attacks and temptations are formulated particularly for you. He is the puppeteer behind all these negative influences we have covered so far, using fear, anxiety, obsessive thinking, and depression as his own assistants to get you to a point of ultimate despair. Think of synchronized swimming and visualize these athletes together creating this beautifully orchestrated production. They are flawless to the point of you forgetting the people that it takes to create such a thing. Now let's say there is one swimmer just flat out messing up and not in alignment with the others. All of a sudden, you just have a pool of people flopping about, and the "trick" has been revealed: that they need each other to create this masterpiece in order for it to visually seem like one. As much as we do not consider depression a "masterpiece," until we realize these negative influences are creating harm, we will just think something is wrong with us, period. Satan wants your mind off these contributing factors behind the curtain and on yourself.

> "For our struggle is not against flesh and blood but against the rulers, against the authorities, against the powers of this dark world and against the spiritual forces of evil in Heavenly realms" (Eph. 6:12).

As far as I was concerned, I had reached rock-bottom during my depression. I was laying by a pool over the summer this year and was thinking about the direction I wanted this book to go. I was trying my best to think of one word that would best describe how I felt during those trying times. Without hesitation, I thought of *saturated*, which is defined as "holding as much water or moisture as can be absorbed; thoroughly soaked." You know how you feel when you get caught in the rain and everything is uncomfortable and your clothes suddenly feel heavy? It makes you feel sluggish due to this new unwanted wet weight. I was saturated with depression and anxiety weighing me down to an unimaginable low. My mind was slowly but habitually turning into a jigsaw puzzle that had to be undone somehow. I remember not even caring about my health, because if I ended up dying, at least I wouldn't feel this way anymore. This is exactly the positioning Satan wants you in as this is what he thinks to be the "end" result of his hard-working antics. I've got news for Satan—it isn't the end and nothing frustrates him more than his plan failing.

As you move further away from this pit, you will feel more resistance caused by him each day. I am going to be honest with you, this section solely about Satan has been the hardest for me to write. Not because of material (I could write a book about him alone), but every interruption you could imagine has occurred. I would sit down to write and the baby would wake up from his nap because my daughter invited the entire neighborhood over, causing the dog to bark and create pure chaos. I have gotten to the point where I literally laugh because it is so obvious, he does not want to be exposed and I can see right through his attempts. Prior to my true knowledge of the devil, I would have totally given up on this book already. "Maybe I am not cut out for this like I first believed. I knew it was just a dream. Blah, blah, blah..."

If you are reading this, then congratulations, you have gotten through the hardest part of your healing process, facing what is underneath. I think we have covered enough about Satan for you to get an idea of who he is and how he is personally affecting you. We will expose him in his hiding places many times throughout this journey. These revelations are not easy to face, but fear not, we have a battle plan that we are about to enter together. And you read that right: *together*. You are not just a number to me. You are a child of God in desperate need of rescuing.

TOOLS

Along with this battle plan, there are some things outside of this book that would help you immensely. I know for myself, people that loved me suggested so many helpful ideas and at first, I viewed it all as more "work." It may seem very tedious at the time, but I promise that each and every one of these things will benefit you in some way! I will list them below:

1. *Attend a church*: It may be hard to muster the ambition to go to church, but I guarantee that you will not regret it. If you do not have a home church, either ask around or search online for one that best suits your beliefs. Worshipping and hearing the word will refresh you and give hope as you develop this new level of relationship with God. It will also provide support by fellowshipping with others. I found that taking notes during church helped me retain everything better (sometimes in bold and underlined many, many times).Like I mentioned in my testimony, I had developed my desperate need for God during worship in church. All of a sudden, these songs were not just lyrics and music. They mimicked my current life and made sense.

2. *Read the Bible*: The Bible can be overwhelming if you do not know where to start. I found it very helpful to search in a Bible concordance for key words. I would look for words like "strength, thoughts, suffering, etc." Some translations are difficult to read, so I usually stick to NLT or NIV. A daily devotional is also very helpful in terms of navigating through the Bible while studying one particular thing at a time.

3. *Worship music*: While I was in Disney World a week into my depression, I actually still needed distraction from the way I felt. I thought for sure my favorite place would do the job, but it didn't. I was surrounded by people running around happy as can be, and it magnified my hopelessness. I had a friend sending me Christian worship music to my email during the vacation, and I would escape to help my desperation. I remember going to the beach and laying in a hammock listening to these songs while looking up into the night sky. It was like the depression couldn't touch me while I played this music, and I clung to that. If you do not know where to start, search for a local Christian station.

4. *Watching/listening to sermons*: At first it was hard for me to get out of the house feeling the way I felt. I knew I had to strengthen my relationship with God in order to start healing, so I started watching Christian pastors from home. I found that I personally gained ground the most in my walk with God by watching Joyce Meyer. Like many pastors, she has many resources including television, online, books, CDs, etc. I would watch her first thing in the morning and I would take notes. Jotting down Bible verses helps strengthen your knowledge of the word eventually making it become a subconscious, spiritually led habit in your life.

5. *Journaling*: As soon as someone suggested this to me, I felt childish-like I had to write in a diary to cope with life. Now looking back, I see how amazing journaling can be! I would date it at the top and write down how I felt that day, what I ate, if I exercised, my scary thoughts, Bible verses, what made me feel better, etc. I would make sure to write down when I felt even the least bit better, by saying "I am getting better." You will have days where you will need to have written proof of times you felt better because this is a bit of a roller coaster ride. It is hard not to get frustrated when you feel that you are starting back at square-one, but all you have to do is look back and see you are making baby steps toward your breakthrough. I go back and read about

what was giving me so much fear. Then I giggle at how silly it is now. I am not underestimating how you are currently feeling, but it's a great place to be when you have overcome a fear that tried to swallow you. If you don't know what to start with, my first page is a list of my blessings. I was told to "make sure to count your blessings" by so many people. It's hard when you are depressed because you have that tunnel vision and you sometimes overlook all your blessings unfortunately. Try to think of some, as we are about to overcome evil with good! I started noticing I was more anxious and depressed when I was bored, so I also made a list of things to do when I felt that way to distract myself from my negative thinking.

6. *Talking with a loved one*: I was blessed enough to have my father help deflate my scary thoughts and guide me through the rough waters of depression. Sometimes it just helps to talk to someone about what you are going through and let it all out. It is important to share these things with someone you trust enough to be positive about your situation. Not everyone has been through depression and anxiety, and sometimes people give bad advice out of the goodness of their heart. Some may say things like: "Rub some dirt in it, you don't have it that bad!" Or, "Just stop thinking about it." If anyone is headed in this direction, then try to find someone that understands. Unfortunately, more people have been through anxiety and depression than you know. Once you open up about what you are going through, you will notice people telling you all about their experiences that you never even knew happened. It is hard not to seem selfish when you are depressed because you are so desperate that it creates a sense of dependency. You will cling to anyone who will comfort you, and that is okay, but remember people can only get you so far in your healing process. God is stripping you of all of your earthly comforts so that you are clinging solely to Him to ultimately heal

you. People cannot physically heal our minds, but we can view them as helpful guides along the way.

7. *Therapist/Christian counselor*: Like the journaling idea, I was very leery of seeking a professional therapist. Therapists or counselors are trained to listen and aid you according to the way your brain specifically functions. I was embarrassed at first and kept it a secret (which is okay by the way) because I didn't want to be viewed as someone going crazy. Again, my biggest scary thought was developing a form of psychosis and being escorted into some institution. My therapist gathered information about my childhood and current situation and explained how things were contributing to the way I was feeling. She was also a Christian therapist and involved God and the Bible in my sessions. This isn't an absolute requirement, but it is very helpful. If money is an issue, a lot of churches provide Christian counselors and are either free or very inexpensive.

Exercise and eating healthily: This might be the hardest thing to motivate yourself to do, especially if you're struggling to get out of bed in the morning. Even just going for a fifteen-minute walk or doing a quick exercise DVD is beneficial. I remember my mom encouraging me to exercise, and I complained about it until I finally gave in. I would be feeling so awful, probably stuck in a viscous scary thought cycle, but the intensity would lessen and I would feel ten times better after. When you exercise, you release chemicals in the brain called endorphins, leaving you to feel "happy" naturally. I have always tried to remember what 1 Corinthians 6:19 says, "Do you not know that your bodies are temples of the Holy Spirit, who is in you, whom you have received from God? You are not your own."

God has blessed us with our bodies and expects us to take the best care we can especially during depression. This also applies to the way we eat as well. When I dove head first into depression, I lost my appetite and got myself to the lowest I have weighed in my adulthood. It wasn't on purpose. I just was not hungry. It may be the opposite for you, some people over eat in order to make themselves feel better. Whichever you may struggle with, know that you will get yourself nowhere with either of these ways of coping. I started eating healthy nutritious foods in small increments slowly. Once my battle plan was on a roll, my appetite returned to normal, and I maintained a healthy weight.

8. *Reduce caffeine*: It's plain and simple, caffeine gives you "energy," but sometimes not in the best way. I am a big coffee drinker, but I noticed when I was anxious and depressed after drinking a cup of coffee, my anxiety was intensified. When we are focused in such a negative direction, the caffeine will only worsen our situation. The effects of caffeine can mimic a panic attack with jittery motions, racing heart, flighty feelings, etc. I promise that you will be able to welcome your cup of joe with open arms as soon as you learn to control your mind. I highly suggest drinking enough water as well. You will notice a boost in energy.

9. *Sleep*: Make sure you are getting a decent amount of sleep. I noticed if I was low on sleep, my fear and anxiety would worsen. My energy was low, and it made it more difficult to fight my battle as I just wanted to go back to sleep.

10. *Reminder cards*: I started doing this after a friend of mine gave me a couple of uplifting Bible verses on cards. I ended up buying some very vibrant three-by-five cards and started writing down verses or quotes that helped me. I would put them on my mirror, car, or my purse. There have been so many times I would be having a hard day but would run into one of these cards and immediately have an "oh yeah!" moment. Just like the worship music, the depression couldn't touch me when I read these. After a while, you start memorizing the truth and it becomes a spirit-led way of life.

"Then you will know the truth, and the truth will set you free" (John 8:32).

WHAT THE BIBLE SAYS ABOUT THE MIND

For the word of God is alive and active. Sharper than any double-edged sword, it penetrates even to dividing soul and spirit, joints and marrow; It judges the thoughts and attitudes of the heart.

—Hebrews 4:12

First of all, isn't the Word amazing? What other book contains love, guidance, and stories that are specifically written to personally help every single human born on this earth? I wanted to start off with this verse as an intro to God's Word and how it plays a very important role in our lives. It doesn't matter if you have this verse memorized or if you are reading it for the first time, it applies to you forever. It is living, meaning no matter how much we progress and age in this world, it is still applicable to us. I view verses and stories in the Bible as puzzle pieces that resonate with each other creating this perfect masterpiece that only rings truth. No matter what you are going through in this life, the Bible has it covered. I have been reading the Bible since I was young, and I still discover scripture, or find new meaning and understanding on how it applies to my life. Since our lives are constantly evolving as we age, we will need help and guidance in areas we haven't necessarily studied before, and it will always be there for us. What does God say about the mind? I love the King James Version of 2 Timothy 1:7, which reads, "For God hath not given us the spirit of fear; but of power, and of love, and of a sound *mind*."

When I think of this verse, it immediately changes my wrong thinking into truth. When you accept Jesus as your savior, you gain the Holy Spirit to live within you and guide you through life as you are reminded of these truths:"But the advocate, the Holy Spirit, whom the Father will send in my name, will teach you all things and will *remind* you of everything I have said to you. Peace I leave with you; my peace I give you. I do not give to you as the world gives. Do not let your hearts be troubled and do not be afraid" (John 14:26–27; emphasis added).

"And hope does not put us to shame, because God's love has been poured out into our hearts through the Holy Spirit, who has been given to us" (Rom. 5:5; emphasis added).

The reason you feel so disgusting with depression is because it is the polar opposite of who God is. My daughter has gotten more splinters in her little hands than I can count. You know how much those annoying slivers of wood can hurt—they are not meant to be under our skin. What is so amazing about the human body is it recognizes this fact and can eventually evict the splinter on its own. I would get so frustrated trying to get these things out of my daughter's hands, but my husband would tell me to be patient and allow her body to push it out on its own. Fear within our mind is spiritually foreign, God did not instill in us a spirit of fear when he knit us in our mother's womb. The Holy Spirit has an actual responsibility of reminding you of right thinking and actions in your life, you just need to listen. I have said it multiple times already that we are to create these new thinking patterns that are aligned with the Word of God. Do you see how these puzzle pieces are fitting together? God is our father in heaven whom sent His son Jesus Christ to set an example of how we are to live. When it was time for Jesus to die for our sins and ascend into heaven, we were sent the Holy Spirit. In times of trouble, we are to go to God in prayer, the Bible for written direction with Jesus's example that we are to model ourselves after, and listen for the Holy Spirit's guidance. This is a continual course for the remainder of your life here on earth. So what is the first step in this change in our thinking? Let's check out Romans 12:2:"Do not conform to the pattern of this world, but be transformed by the renewing of your mind. Then you will be able to test and approve what God's will is—his good, pleasing and perfect will."

What we have here is pure hope, "but be transformed by the renewing of your mind." This verse is a huge indicator that God knew way ahead of your struggles that you would need guidance in the area of the mind, and His plan for your healing is already mapped out. God is putting the ball in your court, so to speak. The move is yours to make. While God will remain holding the reins on His end, He is basically saying that you will have some work to do by "renewing your mind." The *Merriam-Webster* dictionary defines *renew* as "making like new: restoring freshness." Our goal here is to constantly be renewing and maintaining our mind. My husband and I recently bought our first home and are so blessed with it, but we are not used to maintaining one. We have rented for the last five years and always had some maintenance guy come to the rescue when something broke. In the last month, we have had issues with our water heater, refrigerator, and dish washer. It's unbelievable the inconvenient times the problems presented themselves as well, but without repairing them, we would have some big problems! I am learning that with constant maintenance and care of our household responsibilities, we have way less of an issue than if we would have just ignored them.

Maintaining helps the impact not be so big and destructive enough to knock us off our feet the next time we encounter a trial. We have a big problem that presents itself in our mind, we learn how to fix the urgent problem, and then we maintain that way of thinking. Renewing is sometimes not an easy task and you are not completely free of hardship, but God didn't leave us hanging by telling us to guess the way, he lovingly provides direction. Renewing is creating good habits that continue on while breaking the old. We have covered all the negative influences that plague our mind. How do we break them? If we were capable of creating these bad habits, then we are more than capable of creating good habits! I love the way that the Amplified Bible reads in Colossians 3:2:"Set your mind and keep focused habitually on the things above [the heavenly things], not on things that are on earth [which have only temporal value.]"

We need a new habit formation in a godly direction, "focused habitually on the things above." This is what we as anxious and depressed people do best. We subconsciously practice bad thinking patterns as they go around and around in our head throughout the day. There are many stories in the Bible that express people struggled with turmoil in their mind, all you have to do is read the book of Psalms and you will see the despair and pleas. One man in the Bible that stands out to me is David. In Psalm 13:1, he wrote,

> How long Lord? Will you forget me forever? How long will you hide your face from me? How long must I wrestle with my thoughts and day after day have sorrow in my heart? How long will my enemy triumph over me? Look on me and answer, Lord my God. Give light to my eyes, or I will sleep in death, and my enemy will say, "I have overcome him." And my foes will rejoice when I fall. But I trust in your unfailing love, my heart rejoices in your salvation. I will sing the Lord's praise, for he has been good to me.

Now, I was under way different circumstances than David, but oh how I can relate to how he felt. Please do not be offended by this because I myself was there as well, but this is an example of victim mentality. This is why we seem selfish to others around us during these trials. Do I blame him for feeling this way? No! We are clingy and desperate for anyone to rescue us from what we think is being *done to us*. Here is the good news: *you are never to be a victim within your own mind, ever*. You are simply allowing these thoughts to overcome, and it's very tricky. Something I never knew I had power over was choosing my own thoughts on purpose. I just let them fall into my mind. The scariest thought would present itself, and I would just let it torment me to no end. It didn't matter what was going on around me. My entire self was held captive in this thought. I would go to bed at night just begging for God to miraculously take this suffering away from me. Then I proceeded to wake up with this immediate racing heart and flighty feeling the next day. Many people joke about feeling like its Groundhog Day, but it does! You start allowing yourself to believe that it will never go away, which is a lie P.S. Visually speaking, I was held as prisoner of my own mind, and I was unknowingly giving Satan consent to allow it to happen. Little did I know, I was a prisoner within the wrong cell.

> "He upholds the cause of the oppressed and
> gives food to the hungry. The Lord sets prisoners
> free" (Ps. 146:7).

RETURN TO YOUR FORTRESS

Return to your fortress, you prisoners of hope; even now I announce that I will restore twice as much to you.

—Zechariah 9:12

This is such an amazing visual of how we are to view hope. We are not to escape from it! Hope is a huge factor in healing, but it's easy to be lost when you are anxious and depressed. Hope is such a broad topic in the Bible. There are many verses that vocalize it without even mentioning the word itself. We should be filled with hope with just the simple promise of eternity in heaven! Obviously, God knew how our minds and hearts could wander or this verse would not even exist. He does not desire us to remain in this anxious filled mind-set. He wants us to reach peace through Him.

"Yes, my soul, find rest in God; my hope comes from him" (Ps. 62:5).

Such a simple verse, but oh-so important. We are encountered by anxiety-driven fear, and we begin this panic that turns into a bad habit. But God provides written direction on how to interrupt this process all over the Bible. At first, I wanted something I could see with my eyes to give me full hope and repair me. I didn't believe something I could not look at could give me this. As I moved through my depression, I became very aware that *only God* could give me this.

> "Now faith is confidence in what we hope
> for and assurance about what we do not see"
> (Heb. 11:1).

So piecing these verses together reminds us to flee to our fortress, be fully engulfed in hope, and find rest and peace from a faithful, loving God and we will be filled with joy!

Well, what exactly is our fortress? Returning to our fortress is returning to God, He is our fortress. Webster Dictionary defines *fortress* as a "fortified place; a stronghold." A *stronghold* is defined as "a place that has been fortified so as to protect it against attack." There are many references to God being a fortress all over the Bible: "He said 'The Lord is my rock, my fortress and my deliverer'" (2 Sam. 22:2).

> "The Lord almighty is with us; the God of
> Jacob is our fortress" (Ps. 46:7).

> "Deliver me from my enemies, O God; be
> my fortress against those who are attacking me"
> (Ps. 59:1).

> "Be my rock of refuge, to which I can always
> go; give the command to save me, for you are my
> rock and my fortress" (Ps. 71:3).

Just like movies set in medieval times, wars between kingdoms were all pretty similar. Usually one kingdom was trying to overtake the other within their own walls. The kingdom on the defense pulls up their draw bridge and braces for impact while hoping to protect themselves. This fortress is strategically designed to take many hits from the enemy, as it was structured with this possibility in mind. Sometimes it's just not looking good for the kingdom on defense, and they are in search of a miracle. It becomes evident that they cannot defeat the enemy without any additional aid. This is typically when the "hero" shows up (most likely Brad Pitt or Tom Cruise) and just completely turns the outcome around single-handedly. The kingdom is saved to everyone's surprise and picks up the pieces as strength and endurance have been gained. This is how we are to react when we need to protect ourselves from the devil's schemes. We must bolt to our fortress at the onset of an attack. Do you think if the kingdom saw the enemy running at them that they would just hang in the courtyard out front and fight there as they improvise? No, they want that fortified, rock-solid protection with a battle plan in mind. Speaking of plans, kingdoms were constantly trying to revise strategic moves with huge maps sprawled out. You've seen it—everyone is sweaty and tired from battle and are all congregating around a map on a table pointing to things with monopoly-like game pieces representing each kingdom. We need a battle plan in mind already prepared for when we are under attack mentally and spiritually.

So, if we are to picture ourselves fleeing to God in times of despair, then we can access hope and turn from our destructive thinking. Do you see how you can do a 180-degreeturn within your mind with this approach? Once you practice this way of thinking over and over, you create a new center where you will have "oh yeah" moments as you read scripture and remember truth. This baseline will help you compare the difference between your desperate anxious mind and your God-filled, solid fortress mind. You can distinguish the bonfire that fear sets off and the more you return to it, the more it will become a natural response.

When we are in such a wretched place mentally, we are easily distracted from what the Word of God says. I too will be having a rough day and have to remind myself of scripture, sometimes out loud if necessary! After I read it, I cannot fathom how I even forgot it in the first place, but I am thankful to remember. Satan essentially wants us to have memory loss, but as you renew your mind, it becomes harder for him to succeed at this. Like I suggested, those reminder cards will come in handy during your battles! Put them on your fridge, dashboard, mirror, anything you look at on a daily basis.

This all sounds good, but how do we get to our own fortress in the first place? Sometimes it's overwhelming to know the exact steps to take, but God will guide you and it's actually pretty simple. We tend to overthink God sometimes and make healing more complex than it really is. Anxious people analyze almost everything they encounter in order to make sense of it. There is a lot of work to be put into your healing, but not complicated work. My husband Chris can be very serious at times when approaching God in prayer, and that is totally fine. It is a personal preference on how it is to be said, but I view prayer as having a constant conversation with God. It's okay if it isn't perfect. Sometimes I will be on the floor of my closet ugly crying while I somehow get out the words of my desperation.

> "In the same way, the Spirit helps us in our weakness. We do not know what we ought to pray for, but the Spirit himself intercedes for us through wordless groans. And he who searches our hearts knows the mind of the Spirit, because the Spirit intercedes for God's people in accordance with the will of God" (Rom. 8:26).

Meanwhile I will ask Chris to say a prayer on the spot and he will take in the request respectfully and ponder in silence on what he wants to say. Again, nothing wrong with this way, just two different ways of praying. My point is, don't think too hard on how to come to God. We can come broken as we are immediately: "Come to me, all you who are weary and burdened, and I will give you rest" (Matt. 11:28)

There is no indication in this verse to clean yourself up before even thinking of bothering God, the weary are welcomed. Some days I feel led to open my Bible or put on some worship music. Other times I will ask a friend for godly advice, or I will walk around the house just having a conversation with God through prayer. No matter what I choose to help me get to my fortress, it always leads me to that bliss-filled hope in God and place of safety in my mind. We know how "safety" is described in society, but what if we defined it solely around God. Psalm 91 does an amazing job at summing it up for us:

Whoever dwells in the shelter of the Most High will rest in the shadow of the Almighty. I will say of the Lord, "He is my refuge and my fortress, my God, in whom I trust." Surely he will save you from the fowler's snare and from the deadly pestilence. He will cover you with his feathers, and under his wings you will find refuge; his faithfulness will be your shield and rampart. You will not fear the terror of the night, nor the arrow that flies by day, nor the pestilence that stalks in the darkness, nor the plague that destroys midday. A thousand may fall by your side, ten thousand at your right hand, but it will not come near you. You will only observe with your eyes and see the punishment of the wicked. If you say, "The Lord is my refuge," and you make the Most High your dwelling, no harm will overtake you, no disaster will come near your tent. For he will command his angels concerning you to guard you in all your ways; they will lift you up in their hands, so that you will not strike your foot against a stone. You will tread on the lion and the cobra; you will trample the great lion and the serpent. "Because he loves me," says the Lord, "I will rescue him; I will protect him, for he acknowledges my name. He will call on me, and I will answer him; I will be with him in trouble, I will deliver him and honor him. With long life I will satisfy him and show him my salvation.(Ps. 91:1–16)

We can't get any more "safe" than that, what a description of protection! You may be a bit confused on the whole idea of rest. Aren't we supposed to be in an ongoing battle against Satan? Should we really be resting at a time like this?

"The Lord will fight for you; you need only to be still" (Exod. 14:14).

We need to raise our "white flag" to God, not our enemy. We cannot win our battles on our own. We desperately need God. Your responsibility is getting to your fortress and following God's guidance. Being still is considered spiritual warfare as you are still fighting your battle while you are resting in God. Surely if you are resting, you aren't anxious or depressed, which is going against Satan's plan. You are at peace and have full trust in God to get you through.

Jehoshaphat defeated his enemy because God fought for him in 2 Chronicles 20:

> After this, the Moabites and Ammonites with some Meunites came to wage war against Jehoshaphat. Some people came and told Jehoshaphat, "A vast army is coming against you from Edom, from the other side of the Dead Sea. It is already in Hazezon Tamar." Alarmed, Jehoshaphat resolved to inquire of the Lord, and he proclaimed a fast for all Judah. The people of Judah came together to seek help from the Lord; indeed, they came from every town in Judah to seek him. Then Jehoshaphat stood up in the assembly of Judah and Jerusalem at the temple of the Lord in the front of the new courtyard and said: "Lord, the God of our ancestors, are you not the God in Heaven? You rule over the kingdoms of the nations. Power and might are in your hand, and no one can withstand you. Our God, did you not drive out the inhabitants of this land before your people Israel and give it forever to the decedents of Abraham your friend? They have lived in it and have built in it a sanctuary for your Name, saying, 'If calamity comes upon us, whether the sword of judgement, or plague or

famine, we will stand in your presence before this temple that bears your Name and will cry out to you in our distress, and you will hear and save us.' "But now here are men from Ammon, Moab and mount Seir, whose territory you would not allow Israel to invade when they came from Egypt; so, they turned away from them and did not destroy them. See how they are repaying us by coming to drive us out of the possession you gave us as an inheritance. Our God, will you not judge them? For we have no power to face this vast army that is attacking us. We do not know what to do but our eyes are on you." All the men of Judah, with their wives and children and little ones, stood there before the Lord…" "Listen, King Jehoshaphat and all who live in Judah and Jerusalem! This is what the Lord says to you: 'Do not be afraid or discouraged because of this vast army. For the battle is not yours, *but God's*. Tomorrow march down against them. They will be climbing up by the pass of Ziz, and you will find them at the end of the gorge in the Desert of Jeruel. *You will not have to fight this battle*. Take up your possessions; stand firm and see the deliverance the Lord will give you, Judah and Jerusalem. Do not be afraid; do not be discouraged. Go out to face them tomorrow, and the Lord will be with you." (2 Chron. 20:1–17; emphasis added)

This is physically identical to our medieval example of fleeing to our fortress when a threatening enemy is on its way. Jehoshaphat approaches God and cries out in distress for the people of Judah. He is putting up his white flag of surrender to God while admitting that it is out of their power as an army to withstand the enemy alone. He also humbly admits that they do not know what to do, which allows God's will to enter into the situation. I cannot tell you how many times I have gotten on my knees in midst of a storm saying, "God, I don't know what to do, please help me. I can't do this alone." God showed up for Judah just in time:

> Early in the morning they left for the Desert of Tekoz. As they set out, Jehoshaphat stood and said, "Listen to me, Judah and people of Jerusalem. Have faith in the Lord your God and you will be upheld; have faith in his prophets and you will be successful." After consulting the people, Jehoshaphat appointed men to sing to the Lord and to praise him for the splendor of his holiness as they went out at the head of the army, saying: "Give thanks to the Lord for his love endures forever." As they began to sing and praise, the Lord set ambushes against the men of Ammon and Moab and Mount Seir who were invading Judah, and they were defeated. The Ammonites and Moabites rose up against the men from Mount Seir to destroy and annihilate them. After they finished slaughtering the men from Seir, they helped to destroy one another. When the men of Judah came to the place that overlooks the desert and looked toward the vast army, they saw only dead bodies lying on the ground; no one had escaped. So, Jehoshaphat and his men went to carry off their plunder, and they found among them a great amount of equipment and clothing and also articles of value—more than they could take away. There was so much plunder that it took three days to collect it. On the fourth day, they assembled in the Valley of Berakah, where they praised the Lord. This is why it is called the Valley of Berakah to this day. Then, led by Jehoshaphat, all the men of Judah and Jerusalem returned joyfully to Jerusalem, for

the Lord had given them cause to rejoice over their enemies. They entered Jerusalem and went to the temple of the Lord with harps and lyres and trumpets. The fear of God came on all the surrounding kingdoms when they heard how the Lord had fought against the enemies of Israel. *And the kingdom of Jehoshaphat was at peace, for his God had given him rest on every side.* (2 Chron. 20:20–30; emphasis added)

Not only did God step in and fight for Judah, but he gave them rest, then blessed them beyond their dreams. It would have been enough to save them from their enemy, but He continued to provide and love them even after their request was fully met. Doesn't rest on every side sound so amazing? To me, this means that nothing went unnoticed. They were held safely within a fortified place. This wasn't the story prior to God fighting for Judah. There was threatening pressure on all sides! We see this also in 2 Corinthians 4:8 (emphasis added): "We are hard pressed on every side, but not crushed; perplexed, *but not in despair*; persecuted, *but not abandoned*, struck down, *but not destroyed*."

Just like these physical battles, we have spiritual battles on a daily basis. One battle I wrestle with is being the right mother for my children. There are days I do not think I am going to make it without collapsing. These kids are amazing, and I know I am so blessed with them, but I am sometimes left feeling defeated. Now, this is a common feeling parents have at times and it is totally normal, but it can still make you feel alone. When you are exhausted and believing every lie Satan throws at you, it is easy to get stuck in a sticky web. Fearful thoughts can actually make you physically cower, just like you would in an actual battle. So picture me crying on the floor in my closet after a long day with the kids, and I'm just beside myself. Thoughts of not being good enough are just ablaze in my head and I am falling for every trap set. Now, I have been practicing renewing my mind for a while now, but sometimes it takes some effort getting me there. I will realize the path my mind is taking, and all of a sudden, I will start getting the energy I need to flee to my fortress. This is when the Holy Spirit shows up and gives you a little nudge in the right direction. Remember John 14:26 talked about the Holy Spirit being your advocate? Isaiah 11:2 says, "The Spirit of the Lord will rest on him- the Spirit of wisdom and of understanding, the Spirit of counsel and of might, the Spirit of the knowledge and fear of the Lord."

Scripture will be put on your heart and you will begin talking yourself out of the pit you are quickly slipping into. With every verse we remember or worship song we listen to, we get closer to our fortress. Our mind can be utilized as a temptation breeding ground and we just allow our fear to multiply subconsciously. In my example, I am tempted to believe these lies from the devil and follow his path of self-destruction as a failing mother. But 1 Corinthians 10:13 says, "No temptation has overcome you except what is common to mankind. And God is faithful; he will not let you be tempted beyond what you can bear. But when you are tempted, he will also provide a way out so that you can endure it."

Then, I would recall Philippians 4:13:"I can do all things through Christ who strengthens me."

Lastly, I would remember Deuteronomy 31:8:"The Lord himself goes before you and will be with you; he will never leave you nor forsake you. Do not be afraid; do not be discouraged."

With these three verses, I remind myself that this hard time will not overcome me. God is faithful in his promise to not give me more than I can handle because I can do all things through Christ who strengthens me. I am told not to be afraid because God goes before me and will never leave or forsake me. God knew before He blessed me with my children that I was the exact mother they needed with His help or he would not have given them to me in the first place. Sometimes this is all it will take and boom! I am in my fortress filling up with reminders of God's Word and promises. My joy and peace follow right behind, and I have now gained enough strength to move on with my day. Fear, anxiety, and depression have been evicted from my mind for the time being, but I stay armored for there will be more attacks on the horizon.

STAYING ARMORED

We have covered when we must flee to our fortress during times of despair, but what about what we do on a consistent basis? I've given you the example of the medieval way of always being prepared for battle, but what about a present-day example? Staying armored is not only for your mind internally but it's for external uncontrollable circumstances as well. When the attacks of 9/11 occurred, people were flocking to churches and finally coming to God out of fear. Now, of course, this is not a bad thing, because not everyone finds God the same way. People were so scared of repetitive attacks that they needed security in something other than themselves and earthly things. Even people that had already believed in God but had strayed away were coming to Him out of pure panic. Unfortunately for some, this was just a temporary comfort that helped them get through a scary time, but when things started looking up and seeming under control, God was no longer necessary. What took me so long to understand is that this needed to be a constant daily way to live no matter what my circumstances were. Not only is it amazing to have a relationship with God, but when we are consistent, attacks on the mind that come in the future are nowhere near as detrimental.

SIN

We are armored when we are on top of our sin, maintaining this area is crucial to recovery. We live in a fallen world, and we are all sinners. When my depression first hit, I thought it was God's way of punishing me for falling off my path that led to Him. I was mixed into the wrong crowd that thrived on swearing, treating people poorly, drinking, etc. I knew it wasn't right while I was involved, but I ignored the Holy Spirit. Just like the splinter example, this lifestyle did not match Jesus, and it needed to come to an end. God wasn't punishing me by "giving" me depression. He probably had tried many times to get my attention to aid me out of that mess, but I chose to ignore. God allowed me to go through this, and He was giving me nudges so I would get back on the right path. The more I ignored, the more intense the nudges were. It eventually turned my eyes on Him because I knew I couldn't conquer my sin on my own. God sees ahead of us, and He knows our potential. He wants to bless you in your purpose in this world. So, if there is any consistent sin in your life that you are feeling convicted of, go to God and ask Him to guide you out of it. This sin may be holding you captive in your mind, and maybe that is where your obsession and anxiety stem from. We are obsessive thinkers. We can easily slip into forming an addiction of our sin, making us prisoners of it.

"For I see that you are full of bitterness and
captive to sin" (Acts 8:24).

But there is so much hope in breaking the chains of a persistent sin! This is lengthy, but so important:

55

What shall we say, then? Shall we go on sinning so that grace may increase? By no means! We are those who have died to sin; how can we live in it any longer? Or don't you know that all of us who were baptized into Christ Jesus were baptized into his death? We were therefore buried with him through baptism into death in order that, just as Christ was raised from the dead through the glory of the Father, we too may live a new life. For if we have been united with him in a death like his, we will certainly also be united with him in a resurrection like his. For we know that our old self was crucified with him so that the body ruled by sin might be done away with, that we should no longer be slaves to sin— because anyone who has died has been set free from sin. Now if we died with Christ, we believe that we will also live with him. For we know that since Christ was raised from the dead he cannot die again; death no longer has mastery over him. The death he died, he died to sin once for all; but the life he lives, he lives to God. In the same way, count yourselves dead to sin but alive to God in Christ Jesus. Therefore, do not let sin reign in your mortal body so that you obey its evil desires. Do not offer any part of yourself to sin as an instrument of wickedness, but rather offer yourselves to God as those who have been brought from death to life; and offer every part of yourself to him as an instrument of righteousness. For sin shall no longer be your master, because you are not under the law, but under grace. What then? Shall we sin because we are not under the law but under grace? By no means! Don't you know that when you offer yourselves to someone as obedient slaves, you are slaves of the one you obey- whether you are slaves to sin which leads to death, or to obedience, which leads to righteousness? But thanks be to God that, though you used to be slaves to sin, you have come to obey from your heart the pattern of teaching that has now claimed your allegiance. You have been set free from sin and have become slaves to righteousness. I am using an example from everyday life because of your human limitations. Just as you used to offer yourselves as slaves to impurity and to ever increasing wickedness, so now offer yourselves as slaves to righteousness leading to holiness. When you were slaves to sin, you were free from the control of righteousness. What benefit did you reap at that time from the things you are now ashamed of? Those things result in death! But now that you have been set free from sin and have become slaves of God, the benefit you reap leads to holiness, and the result is eternal life. For the wages of sin is death, but the gift of God is eternal life in Christ Jesus our Lord. (Rom. 6:1–23)

A lot of repetition, but we are renewing our minds. We need to crave consistent reminders! Allow the godly repetitions to consume room in your mind and replace the negative. See, we are no longer made to be slaves of sin! I watched a show with my husband once, and there were slaves rowing a big ship in the ocean. They were whipped, malnourished, hungry, thirsty, sunburned, you name it. Very rough conditions as they were chained to their seats to avoid escape. They were physically and mentally stuck and it was making them feel like they were going crazy. They just longed-for land. Now here we are, allowing ourselves to be slaves to sin when we are told we are free from sin! That is like these slaves on the boat knowing that they could be free of this retched lifestyle, but staying there by choice. Get to your fortress, focus on your conviction you are feeling and allow God to help you break the chains to the sin you will no longer be a slave to!

"For I will forgive their wickedness and will remember their sins no more" (Heb. 8:12).

HE IS ALL WE NEED

I remember about midway through my depression. I was starting to feel much better and I saw the light at the end of the tunnel. I was working hard on my fears, anxiety, depression, and sin diligently. I had formed a new way of living centered on God, and I was so immersed in His word. This new relationship I had with Him was nothing I had experienced before. I craved it like I needed it to survive, and it was proving to be what was getting me through. God had allowed me to be completely stripped of everything of this earth that brought me comfort and security so that my eyes were on him. I was now in full realization that God was all I needed and the rest would follow after. What exactly did he strip me of? Doesn't he want me to enjoy my life and have these things? Well, sometimes we need to get to a point where earthly comforts aren't enough because they cannot fully satisfy us:

> "I will refresh the weary and satisfy the faint" (Jer. 31:25).

> "You open your hand and satisfy the desires of every living thing" (Ps. 145:16).

> "Satisfy us in the morning with your unfailing love that we may sing for joy and be glad all our days" (Ps. 90:14).

> "The Lord will guide you always; he will satisfy your needs in a sun-scorched land and will

strengthen your frame. You will be like a well-watered garden, like a spring whose waters never fail" (Isa. 58:11).

During my depression, I mentioned I had to quit my job, my friends lost interest in being around me, my parents could not fix me, and I no longer felt joy in things I typically loved. These are the things God allowed me to temporarily lose in order to completely have all focus on Him. He wanted me to fully lean on and trust Him to get me out of this nightmare. For only He could fully satisfy me. Losing these things are not what I want to happen to you, but sometimes it takes that wake-up call if you aren't listening to the Holy Spirit. I was being stubborn and thought it was such a sacrifice to give up my old self—it hurt. An outsider can view this and think, "Won't that make someone even more depressed?" Well, yeah, of course it can, if they don't have God. I made it because of God. I got through to the other side and He has blessed me beyond what I deserve. I made new friends, got a better job, became married to an amazing man, had children, and entered into a whole new journey with a testimony to help others.

"But first and most importantly seek [aim at, strive after] His kingdom and his righteousness [His way of doing and being right—the attitude and character of God], and *all these things will be given to you also*" (Matt. 6:33, AMP; emphasis added).

Individuals that struggle with anxiety tend to find that it eases their mind to have a daily routine. I believe that mentally it makes one feel that they at least have control in something. I had reached a point of waking up thinking of God, reading His word, listening to worship music, watching sermons, journaling about my journey, etc. Because I was so desperate in my state of depression and this seemed to be the only thing getting me through, I clung to it and was committed. I woke up one morning feeling amazing, and I caught myself actually thinking, "Maybe I'm fully recovered and I don't need to get too into my routine today." The attacks on my mind had seemed to be tapering off a little, and I was relaxed. I felt myself tempted to just go back to the way I was living since I was "good" now. Maybe reading my Bible here and there, but not as a regiment. This temptation was obviously conducted by Satan, and I am sure this preterm recovery would have only lasted so long. I am so thankful that I caught this early on, recognized the maker, and opposed it. Doing this brought to light what the illusion from Satan was trying to hide: my daily need for God. Some may think I was crazy for what I did next, but that's okay, I felt it on my heart from God. I actually prayed out loud to be desperate for God again out of fear of losing this new-found need for Him. What I didn't understand yet was that I was praying to be tested, and God followed through.

"Search me, God, and know my heart: test
me and know my anxious thoughts" (Ps. 139:23).

The following day I felt the worst I had experienced the entire journey. I entered a whole new level of maturity in this test, and I lived to tell! Now this doesn't mean we should pray for harm to come onto us as a punishment, or that God is trying to make us feel bad. I was trying to allow my flesh to see what my spirit already knew, that God is to be sought out and desired in our heart daily because we love Him, not because we just need him in times of trouble.

Let's camp back at the visual we had going of the kingdoms during battle. When we picture a knight, they aren't just vulnerably walking around in their street clothes, they are head-to-toe in armor. They have helmets, chest plates, shields, swords, etc. The only exposed portion of their body are their eyes, which peek through tiny slits in their helmet. We all know it is crucial to be able to at least see our opponent, but everything else is protected heavily.

Finally, be strong in the Lord and in his
mighty power. Put on the full armor of God, so
that you can take your stand against the devil's

schemes. For our struggle is not against flesh and blood, but against the rulers, against the authorities, against the powers of this dark world and against the spiritual forces of evil in the Heavenly realms. Therefore, put on the full armor of God, so that when the day of evil comes, you may be able to stand your ground, and after you have done everything to stand. Stand firm then, with the belt of truth buckled around your waist, with the breastplate of righteousness in place, and with your feet fitted with the readiness that comes from the gospel of peace. In addition to all of this take up the shield of faith, with which you can extinguish all the flaming arrows of the evil one. Take the helmet of salvation and the sword of the spirit which is the word of God. And pray in the Spirit on all occasions with all kinds of prayers and requests. With this in mind, be alert and always keep on praying for all the Lord's people. (Eph. 6:10).

Not only are we desired to keep our loving relationship strong with God, but we are also to be consistent in protecting ourselves from these attacks. If we protect ourselves daily on the offense, we will not be found on the defense. It is such a threat to Satan when we follow this plan, because he knows the power and authority God holds. We have confirmation on where God stands in John 16:33:"I have told you these things, so that in me you may have peace. In this world, you will have trouble. But take heart! I have overcome the world!"

Jesus has already overcome the world; the battle has already been won for us! He has no equal, and no one compares, not even Satan.

"The great dragon was hurled down- that ancient serpent called the devil, or Satan, who leads the whole world astray. He was hurled to the earth, and his angels with him" (Rev. 12:9).

Jesus also speaks on where Satan landed in Luke 10:17–20:

> The seventy-two returned with joy and said, "Lord, even the demons submit to us in your name." He (Jesus) replied, "I saw Satan fall like lightning from Heaven. I have given you authority to trample on snakes and scorpions and to overcome all the power of the enemy; nothing will harm you. However, do not rejoice that the spirits submit to you, but rejoice that your names are written in Heaven."

God has power and authority, while Satan only holds power that does not exceed God's.

"Does Job fear God for nothing?" Satan replied. Have you not put a hedge around him and his household and everything he has? You have blessed the work of his hands so that his flocks and herds are spread throughout the land. But now stretch out your hand and strike everything he has, and he will surely curse you to your face." The Lord said to Satan, "Very well, then, everything he has is in your power, but on the man himself do not lay a finger" (Job 1:9).

We have already gone over the end to Job's story, and he won his battle because of his strong faith and endurance. Satan had power to cause these terrible conditions for Job, but God already knew the outcome and Job passed his test because he held authority over Satan's power. I think the capability of possessing authority over our oppressor is a blessed gift from God. This means we have authority over what occurs in our mind including fear, anxiety, depression, temptations, etc. Every single arrow that Satan throws at you is to be managed by you with the help of God. Your authority trumps his power, making his attacks spiritually ineffective. So, on your hardest day, remember that the darkness of Satan will never encompass you if you have God, never. We are given this reminder in Romans 8:31:

"What, then, shall we say in response to these things? If God is for us who can be against us."

As you are crawling in agony to your fortress for the millionth time, remember that you will still win your battle because of what Jesus has already accomplished for us by dying on the cross. Satan tried everything he could possibly think of to harm Jesus on earth. We have already discussed the temptations he threw at Jesus, but he also tried other tactics after failing:"Jesus answered, "I tell you, Peter, before the rooster crows today, you will deny three times that you know me" (Luke 22:34).

> It was just before the Passover Festival. Jesus knew that the hour had come for him to leave this world and go to the Father. Having loved his own who were in the world, he loved them to the end. The evening meal was in progress and the devil had already prompted Judas, the son of Simon Iscariot to betray Jesus. Jesus knew that the Father had put all things under his power, and that he had come from God and was returning to God... Jesus was troubled in spirit and testified, "Very truly I tell you, one of you is going to betray me." His disciples stared at one another, at loss to know which of them he meant...Leaning back against Jesus, he asked him, "Lord who is it?" Jesus answered, "It is the one whom I will give this piece of bread when I have dipped it in the dish. Then, dipping the piece of bread, he gave it to Judas, the son of Simon Iscariot. As soon as Judas took the bread, Satan entered into him.(John 13:1–3, 21, 22–27)

Just like the kingdom on the defense was not looking hopeful to the human eye, Jesus's future seemed to be grim. Satan persuaded Peter, a very close disciple and friend of Jesus to deny him three times. He also had Judas turn Jesus in to be crucified for meaningless greed.

This is when we need that hero to come to our rescue, our Almighty Father. God goes before us and had this already planned out, making Satan no match for Him. Even with all of these plans the evil one concocted, he still was defeated. God gave Satan the ultimate black eye by using Satan's evil tactics to his advantage and turning them into good: "You intended to harm me, *but God* intended it for good to accomplish what is now being done, the saving of many lives" (Gen. 50:20).

> "And we know that in all things God works for the good of those who love him, who have been called according to his purpose" (Rom. 8:28).

Not only did the enemy not accomplish what he desired, God turned it into good by the death of our sins on the cross and the resurrection of Jesus Christ. I also want to look back and touch on another point in Luke 10:20, "Do not rejoice that the spirits submit to you, but rejoice that your names are written in Heaven." The way I view this is, "Let's not get too distracted to the point of forgetting what is important." Because of Jesus dying on the cross for our sins, heaven is promised to us when we accept Him as our Lord and Savior. Jesus is definitely encouraging us to have authority over Satan, but not to dwell on it and lose our sight of eternal life in Heaven. In the game of football, "celebrating" at the end zone is highly frowned upon. These players score a touchdown and proceed to do backflips followed by dancing. Basically, they are saying, "Look what I can do!" This is such a distraction. Even coaches get annoyed because their focus is the end result of the game, to win. Although it is necessary to defeat the opposing team, scoring a touchdown does not mean you win the game and forget the rest of the challenge. We need a repetition in scoring against Satan without distractions and with our eyes on our eternal prize—heaven.

ACCESSING OUR AUTHORITY

Submit yourselves, then, to God. Resist the devil, and he will flee from you.

—James 4:7

Resisting the devil is resisting fear, depression, anxiety, tempta-tion, scary thoughts, everything that he represents. How do we know what is from Satan? If it is not in agreeance with the word of God, then it is not from God. We have already covered how Jesus handled Satan's temptations, He said things sternly out loud like "Get behind me Satan" and "It is written." By saying these things, Jesus is claiming his authority in the formation of commands. Satan was badgering Jesus like an obnoxious bully, and Jesus orders him to get out the way of God's will. There is so much power in these words yet they are so simple. Jesus is challenging Satan with a Word of God fact-check here. He too had to go to his fortress and remind Satan of truth to dissolve temptation and make him flee. I have said both of these things out loud many, many times. It's just a great way to call Satan out and expose him mid-attack. When you reach this level of maturity and speak scripture out loud sternly you will feel victory in your battle very quickly. This applies to such a broad spectrum in our lives and can be used for anything you encounter. You can be under attack, flee to your fortress by finding scripture on your situation and there you have it, "It is written." End attack, cue closing credits.

We are called to be the head and not the tail in Deuteronomy 28:13:"The Lord will make you the head, not the tail. If you pay attention to the commands of the Lord your God that I give you this day and carefully follow them, you will always be at the top, never the bottom."

Satan does not have the authority to be above or in front of you, God goes before us and makes us the head and not the tail. I always feel bad for the person in the back end of a horse costume—how on earth do they know where they are going? They just follow the person in the front and hope for the best. We are talking huge trust here in this scenario. Satan cannot be in the front end of your horse costume. That is where you belong so you can see and follow God. So, during your next attack, visualize yourself forcing Satan to get back behind you as you say, "Get behind me, Satan!" I don't care how many times you have to say it, make sure you succeed in making him flee. Get to your fortress!

BATTLE PLAN

I am now going to break up the specific negative influences we are going to dissect according to the word of God, as they each have their own unique way of being overcome. Now is the time, if you haven't gotten there yet, to get angry at how much you are allowing Satan to have power over your mind. I don't want you to be angry with yourself. We are not our own enemy. We have been deceived into thinking something is wrong with us and we will never escape this destroying and dangerous pit. Allow your anger to motivate you into chasing your breakthrough and healing. It is time to claim your authoritative position and become the offense in this battle. Let's catch Satan off guard!

ATTACKING FEAR

Even though I walk through the darkest valley, I will fear no evil, for you are with me; your rod and your staff, they comfort me.

—Psalm 23:4

Just like pulling a weed out of your garden, you need the roots to fully come out or you better expect that weed again, and they grow fast! Fear is the root of depression and anxiety. A good acronym I still remind myself is that *fear* is "false evidence appearing real." Now I know this isn't straight from a Bible verse, but it helps you cognitively grasp a better perspective of the reality of fear. We are exposed to fear the minute we arrive outside of the womb with a loud wail. This wail is expected by everyone in the room, or it could mean something is wrong with the baby. So far, all the baby has experienced is the warm and pleasant (not for mom) home they have been given inside the womb. Noise has been muffled, not much light, and they are just floating in there safe and sound. All of a sudden, they storm unexpectedly into a cold, loud, and unfamiliar room experiencing sight outside of the womb for the first time. The baby is fearful of their environment, so they scream to the best of their ability. Change has come drastically, and it has taken the baby by surprise. They are soon wrapped in warm blankets and are placed back with all they know, their mother. Fear has tapered off, and they grow trust in those caring for them.

So we see here that fear is human nature and we are confronted with it pretty early on. I think this is why I clung to my mother so tightly when depression introduced itself. This new fear was out of her hands. It was for God and I to handle together, and that petrified me. If I could draw up an illustration during this realization, it would be the ground beneath me being swept away as my mom is without a lifesaver. I remember her telling me, "Just stop thinking about it. You can do this. You are so strong." I totally appreciated these words of encouragement, but I could just feel the pressure on myself when I just wanted her to take it away. I felt like complete garbage. I wasn't strong and surely couldn't just stop thinking about anything terrible. This is the space we add God into our healing equation, and it's a big space. While the ones that love us will go great lengths to see us get to our breakthrough, it will never be enough without God.

My daughter is currently six and quite sassy at times. This is very typical but I sometimes take things personally and I find myself ugly crying again on my bathroom floor (surprise, surprise). Before I remember to get to my fortress I usually feed my flesh and become pretty self-centered. "After all that I do for her, does she not know how much she hurts my feelings?" Then I usually come to a point of realization that she is only six and that I need to chill out a bit. I find myself in the land of failure and blame: "I failed her, and she is like this because I'm not doing anything right!" Sometimes I also dip a bit into the land of comparison: "So and so's kids would never be this way, probably because they discipline differently." You get my drift? This is Satan's playground. Anyway, the other day after a mommy failure episode I casted myself in, my daughter was in the back seat singing words to the worship song I had on. She then started singing louder and louder with her eyes closed as she entered her own little time of worship. When it was finished, she told me, "Mommy, when I am having a hard day in school I sing this song to God and it helps me so much!" Cue the waterworks and just sigh of relief, she is not a disaster because of me after all! I am going to fail her so many times, and there are going to be some things in her life I cannot physically help for her. The extent of my aid is taking the best care I can for her and prayer, that's all I can do as her mother. But God will never fail her and he will step in just like He did with the worship song. He will calm her fears when I can't. She got to her fortress at six. God is good!

> "I sought the Lord, and he answered me; he
> delivered me from all my fears" (Ps. 34:4).

ATTACKING WHAT-IF THINKING

But in that coming day no weapon turned against you will succeed. You will silence every voice raised up to accuse you. These benefits are enjoyed by the servants of the Lord; their vindication will come from me. I, the Lord, have spoken!

—Isaiah 54:17

As we have mentioned, what-if thinking is born through a particular fear and can torment you for as long as you allow. I have already given the examples of Jesus saying, "It is written," or "Get behind me, Satan!" When it comes to what-if thinking, we must hit it head on before it multiplies and takes us down an undesirable road. Sometimes I can feel a what-if thought coming at me, so I position myself on the offense and meet it with some back up. We anxious individuals analyze the facts beyond what we need to. Sometimes even the facts aren't enough to stop us from worrying. There have been plenty of times that I have gone into the doctor with a health scare and have walked out with a clean bill of health after great test results. I will be relieved at first, but my brain begins to struggle because my fear has been battled by medical evidence and has lost. About a week after this good news, I will either worry that the doctor missed something, or I will move on to a new ailment. Obviously, this opposition to truth is Satan's doing, and we can call him out like Jesus did. I have a few things I say out loud and remember by heart so that I am already prepared. It's in my battle plan. This would be a great opportunity to use your reminder cards! When I come to Satan's orchestrated attack, I can fight without even getting so worked up. Saying these truths from the Word get me into my fortress and can provide an easy exit out of a destructive plan. We will call these what-if mic drops:

- "It is Written": As we have covered, Jesus responded to Satan's attempts to get him to sin against God. By saying this, we are meeting Satan at battle lines with unchanging truth of the word.
- "Get behind me, Satan": Again, Jesus responded by saying this to remind Satan of the authority he (Jesus) possessed through God.
- "Even if": Instead of saying "what if," work on your even-ifs. Watch this:

Q: *What if* I am banished to the most distant land under the heavens?

A: "*Even if* you have been banished to the most difficult land under the heavens, from there the Lord your God, will gather you and bring you back" (Deut. 30:4).

Even if I throw up at the amusement park, I will still be safe. It may be embarrassing at first, but I will take care of myself in the hotel room until I am well enough to go home.

- "But God": This is stated many times in the Bible. It's reminding us of God's authority and that He is ultimately in control. He has the final word. You can respond to any scary thought with, "But God."
- "I can do all things through Christ": No matter what trouble has approached you in your trial, God is bigger than it. Nothing is a surprise to Him. He knew what was headed your way when He made you. He sets no one up for failure; therefore, you can do anything with Him because He gives you strength.

ATTACKING ANXIETY

Anxiety weighs down the heart, but a kind word cheers it up.

—Proverbs 12:25

I will never forget the time my daughter asked me to tell her stories about herself as a baby. She was about three years old, and we had just finished reading some books before bedtime. Her eyes were big with wonder as she eagerly waited to hear these magical stories about her baby life. At first, I didn't think anything of it. I started with one about how she tried pulling herself out of her hospital bin at two days old. That the nurses could not keep her swaddled, even in a Velcro swaddle, and that she came out of the womb with her fist in the air. She was gleaming with pure happiness at this point, and she asked for more. I thought of one more, and then I became stumped. I couldn't figure it out—why could I not remember more easily? I was put on the spot, but surely as her mother I should know these by heart, she was my world. In that moment, the answer came to me quite quickly, followed by a rush of tears. I had spent the first year of my daughter's life in constant anxiety and obsessive thinking. You see these "scary thoughts" plagued my present moment and replaced my joy with fear. I allowed this to happen, and I am left with not the best memory of the good times. If I look at pictures, I will remember things easily, but off the top of my head, I have to do some digging. I can tell you every single one of my scary thoughts and where I hid in the house to cry when they were overcoming me. I can look at a family picture and remember the exact fear that was nagging me, and

OUT OF THE PIT

that I just wanted the day to be over because I was so sick of feeling so badly. This revelation hit me hard, and I felt like so much was stolen from me. I missed out on many things I could have easily enjoyed, which we now know is Satan's goal. Now that I am on the other side of this and my daughter is almost seven, I would love for nothing more than to go back and do it differently. I think back to these times and wonder why I was so worried. These things that were tormenting me were not even rational thoughts.

> "What do people get for all the toil and anxious striving with which they labor under the sun? All their days their work is grief and pain; even at night their minds do not rest. This too is meaningless" (Eccles.2:22–23).

Each time I had gone through a big chunk of obsessive thinking/depression was during a time that my circumstances were unstable. My first encounter with depression was formed around the sadness I experienced from losing my aunt, which birthed many fears as distractions. As for the anxiety that I had while my daughter was a newborn, anyone would say I had reason to be anxious:

My husband had joined the navy when we first had started dating, and we got married quickly after. We had met each other years before while on the Disney College Program and had gone our separate ways until we reconnected online. I knew he was the one, so I followed him on his new navy adventure with excitement. We ended up getting married in May and found out we were pregnant in August. My labor with my daughter went smoothly until they told me I needed a C-section due to her size. She came out a healthy 10-lb 7-oz beautiful baby. They wheeled us back to our room and everyone started panicking. All I remember is a bunch of nurses and doctors pushing on my stomach with uncertainty in their eyes. They could not get my uterus to contract back to size, and I was losing a lot of blood. I just remember my husband pacing while holding our daughter and looking pale as a ghost. After an hour or so, they had gotten me to stop bleeding (Praise God!) and we were able to have a relaxing stay in the hospital.

My husband had gotten orders to Norfolk, VA, and we planned on leaving only nine days after the birth of our daughter in Michigan. Looking back, I think I should have waited to heal a little more, but we were excited to get to our new home and be together. We moved into our townhome, and it was all fun and games until I realized I didn't know a soul near me. My husband was gone a lot on his ship and always reminded me, "The navy owns me." He is an amazing father and husband, but it was his duty to follow the navy's orders and that was hard for me to accept. This left me feeling so alone and fearful as I gained pressure on doing a lot of things on my own. I would Skype my parents everyday just to have a conversation with someone that I knew. Maelin was an amazing baby, and I felt so blessed, but being a new parent takes a toll on you mentally and physically. My anxiety for her safety started growing at a rapid pace and my what-ifs multiplied. I was constantly worried about her getting sick, slipping in the tub, choking on some miniscule object, etc. You name it, I worried about it. I literally wouldn't give her a bath unless my husband was home. I think it's only natural for new parents to worry about things they have never experienced before, but not to the point of it controlling your every present moment. As we have already gone over how the mind operates, mine was sounding the alarm. It recognized I was so lonely and worn out that it decided to hand over some distracting scary thoughts that caused anxiety driven distraction.

> "Do not be anxious about anything, but in every situation, by prayer and petition, with thanksgiving, present your requests to God" (Phil. 4:6).

I have already drilled into your mind what our fortress is and why it is so important. It's spoken of here again in this verse, "but in every situation, by prayer and petition, with thanksgiving, present your requests to God." This was written by Paul, a man who had gone through a massive transformation. We won't dive too far into Paul's story, but I'll give you a snippet of his former self. Paul was originally called "Saul" and was not a godly man whatsoever:

> Meanwhile, Saul was still breathing out Murderous threats against the Lord's disciples. He went to the high priest and asked him for letters to the synagogues in Damascus, so that if he found any there who belonged to the Way (Jesus), whether men or women, he might take them as prisoners to Jerusalem. As he neared Damascus on his journey, suddenly a light from heaven flashed around him. He fell to the ground and heard a voice say to him, "Saul, Saul, why do you persecute me?" "Who are you Lord?" Saul asked. "I am Jesus, whom you are persecuting," he replied. "Now get up and go into the city, and you will be told what you must do…" For three days he was blind, and did not eat or drink anything. In Damascus there was a disciple named Ananias. The Lord called to him in a vision, "Ananias!" "Yes Lord He answered. The Lord told him, "Go to the house of Judas on Straight Street and ask for a man from Tarsus named Saul, for he is praying. In a vision he has seen a man named Ananias come and place his hands on him to restore his sight." "Lord," Ananias answered, "I have heard many reports about this man and all the harm he has done to your holy people in Jerusalem. And he has come here with authority from the chief priests to arrest all who call on your name." But the Lord said to Ananias, "Go! This man is my chosen instrument to proclaim my name to the Gentiles and their kings and to the people of Israel. I will show him how much he must suffer for my name." Then Ananias went to the house

and entered it. Placing his hands-on Saul, he said, "Brother Saul, the Lord, who appeared to you on the road as you were coming here—has sent me so that you may see again and be filled with the Holy Spirit." Immediately, something like scales fell from Saul's eyes, and he could see again. He got up and was baptized and after taking some food, he regained strength.(Acts 9:1–19)

Now forgive me for the novel of verses, but this background of Paul was necessary to hear so that you can understand my point. Sometimes when we are so depressed and are told how we are to be, it's common to think, "Easy for you to say, you don't know what I've been through. This cannot imply toward me...blah, blah, blah." I know I thought this way at first, but with every verse I read, I got a little less stubborn and humbler each time. First of all, this story of Saul's transition has anxiety written all over it, and he has every right to speak these words. I mean, we are talking total loss of vision from the God he was persecuting—yikes! Just like my example of Job, I am not trying to belittle our current anxieties and fears, but I would be panic-attacking all over this scenario. What is so amazing is that Paul goes on to spread the Gospel all over and begin the Christian Church.

"The Lord gets his best soldiers out of the highlands of affliction" (Charles Spurgeon).

So I think we can be appreciative of Philippians 4:6 even more knowing that it was written by a man who experienced such anxiety-filled circumstances. It is not a command-filled verse without experience. I love how he threw "with thanksgiving" in there as I am sure he understood how grateful he was to have overcome and change into the man God made him to be. What a turnaround this man had. God made him a leader!

"Jesus looked at them and said, 'With man this is impossible, but with God all things are possible'" (Matt. 19:26).

Paul was murdering the very people of God he was now made to lead. Like Job, Paul's outcome was just not expected. I love that about God. With Him, all things are possible!

All right, so we are already fully aware that we are not to be anxious for anything. How is this even doable? We can't just throw our anxieties into a black hole? The amazing thing about God is He tells us where to "dispose" our anxiety. You have probably heard the phrase *give it to God* before. Well, it is birthed in this verse:"Humble yourselves, therefore, under God's mighty hand, that he may lift you up in due time. Cast all your anxiety on him because he cares for you" (1 Pet. 5:6–7).

I love this verse and how much it speaks to me in times of desperate need. You can come to a place of peace during panic and anxiety with this verse alone, I promise. It took some time for me to get to this place, but I can have anxiety over some fear I have encountered and I will recite this verse and imagine God taking it for me. I then can cognitively move on from that anxiety for the time being and go about my day. *Merriam-Webster* defines *cast* like this: "To cause to move or send forth by throwing." Just like when you cast your line while fishing, you don't want the bait, who needs that? You are trading the bait for a fish. You give God your anxious-filled fear. He willingly takes it then gives back peace in the area of struggle.

We are given another illustration of "giving it to God" here: "Come to me, all you who are weary and burdened, and I will give you rest. Take my yoke upon you and learn from me, for I am gentle and humble in heart, and you will find rest for your souls. For my yoke is easy and my burden is light" (Matt. 11:28).

It wasn't until recently that I learned this verse is not about eggs. Even though the spelling of "yolk and yoke" are different, still seemed like eggs to me. I had a friend tell me what exactly a "yoke" was and it all made sense to me finally. *Merriam-Webster* defines *yoke* as "a wooden bar or a frame by which two work animals [such as oxen] are harnessed at the heads or necks for drawing a plow or load." As you can imagine, very large and strong animals are necessary to pull equipment in order to plow a field. This heavy burden on the animal is a challenge to even something of its size, but it is accomplished. In this verse, Jesus is acknowledging the weight of the world that rests upon us and the weariness it brings when we are carrying it alone. Jesus is offering to share the load with you side by side, and with Him, it is less burdensome. We will still go through trials and tribulations, but with God, we can make it! Such a cool visual of Jesus loving us so much that he brings himself willingly to walk alongside of us. Even when we tire, his burden is light enough to keep going.

> "When I said, 'My foot is slipping,' your unfailing love, Lord, supported me. When anxiety was great within me, your consolation brought me joy" (Ps. 94:18–19).

When we get these anxiety attacks, it can seem impossible to overcome them. They consume your entire day sometimes. This is why so many people struggling with anxiety and depression are so tired that they don't want to get out of bed in the morning. They are physically and mentally drained.

I will even get anxious about little things, like having company over for dinner. I am a people-pleaser, so I want everyone comfortable and happy. We have animals, a dog and two cats to be exact, and they are friendly little guys. The dog is pretty rambunctious at first, but then he calms down and just wants to be your cuddle buddy. The cats like to make themselves known by meowing obnoxiously and laying on our guests with all of their fur floating about. Well, some people just aren't animal people and we understand that, but it makes things complicated while trying to entertain. I will literally feel anxiety attacks approaching over the chaos that is about to unfold, and I just want to avoid the situation all together. Or another example would be my fear over saying something to someone that could have been taken the wrong way. I will wallow in anxiety over it for the rest of the day wondering what they thought. To a person without anxiety, these would be easy fixes and wouldn't even be considered thinking twice of. You put the dog in the kennel, and the cats in the basement. If you think you have offended someone, you explain what you meant and that you were sorry if it was taken the wrong way. Done, what's for dinner? I wouldn't even be thinking about dinner. That would be a cereal night for sure. I am busy having anxiety on my closet floor.

Sometimes I just simply wake up feeling anxious for no apparent reason. It is oh-so temping to just go back to bed, but I know I have to fight back or my whole day will be affected. I almost view it as a race between my fortress and my anxiety. I get ready, blare worship music as loudly as I can, and brew myself some coffee and I beat my anxiety to the finish line. It's all about being on the offense. Establish your place and dig those heels in your footing. Usually I get my kids involved as we repeatedly sing, "This is the day. This is the day that the Lord has made. I will rejoice and be glad in it!" Declare it! These aren't just phony scriptures and songs. They are deep, deep truths that you can speak into your life!

> "This is the day that the Lord has made. We
> will rejoice and be glad in it" (Ps. 188:24).

Like I explained in my example about missing moments in my daughter's first year of life, these are the times I would have been missing out on, things God wanted me to enjoy. Satan is a joy stealer, and he just simply is on a mission to not allow you to have it. I remember when depression started in my life. I had so much anxiety that I didn't have room in my mind to give thought to other things. It totally took up vacancy. Just like that phrase, "I can't get my mind off . . ." The first week into my depression my aunt and uncle brought over their brand-new puppy, which typically would make me squeal in excitement, but I just sat on the couch not even pretending to care. I was going through the motions of the day, but my mind was absorbing depression. I recall telling my dad, "If you drove up with a brand-new red Corvette and handed me the keys, I would not even care enough to want it." This is what we do when anxiety is so persistent and isn't dealt with, it guides us straight into emotionless black holes. If we remain in this state, we are basically a puppet allowing negative influences to choose our feelings and actions. This way of living is quite opposite of what God wants for us. I love the version the amplified bible provides of John 10:10:"The thief comes only in order to steal and kill and destroy. I came that they may *have and enjoy life*, and have it in abundance (to the full, till it overflows.)"

Okay, so we have covered some verses and things to say out loud during an anxiety attack, but what if we need more help in order to get through an attack? This is where our tools come in handy that I have mentioned previously. You do not have to use only my tools. I am sure there are more out there that can help greatly. Just make sure they line up with God and you're good. We don't need to develop any new bad habits with outside negative influences. I am going to create a fictional story as an example of how to utilize these tools by modeling this as a template to help relate to your current situation. I would love to sit with every one of you, hear your story and try to help coach you out of your pit to the best of my ability, but it is physically impossible. This is the next best thing coming from my heart, and my prayer for you is that it helps you with guidance as you match your situation to this story:

Susie is typically a happy-go-lucky lover of God but has suddenly become someone she doesn't recognize. She is halfway through her med student program but starting to question her life. She thought she wanted to be a doctor, but it's not an easy profession to pursue and there is a lot of pressure from those around her to succeed. She will be a third-generation female doctor, and the occupation has always been expected of her. She is starting to question if this is really what she wants to do with her life and fear of failing her family is weighing heavy on her. Not only does she fear the lack of passion, but she is unsure if she will even pass. Her parents have been helping her pay for school, so it is evident they would not only be disappointed in her, but they would be out a lot of money. These fears turn into anxiety attacks causing symptoms of racing heart, sweat, loss of appetite, and loss of interest in things that typically bring Susie joy. This becomes an obsession where scary thoughts form as Susie imagines her disappointing future and what it will cause. What-ifs are all that circle in her head as she just tries her best to get through each day. "*What if* I let my family down," "*What if* I don't know what my identity is," "*What if* I don't end up finding a loving husband because I have been centered on my career?" Susie begins to shut down as she distances herself from her friends, family, and leisurely activities. She has some big choices to make and her mind is quite cloudy with all of this anxiety and depression going on. She has been attending church here and there, but isn't really keeping an ongoing relationship with God. She is just not in the mood. Most days she can't even find the strength to open her shades and get out of her bed.

I am going to stop there before I give us all anxiety over a fictional story! Poor Susie has been hit with anxiety and depression, and she is struggling to come up with a solution. We learn that Susie is a Christian but doesn't seem to be in the best relationship with God. It seems that she is allowing her circumstances to control how she feels as she is losing what typically brings her joy. Several people I have tried to help have told me, "I thought about reading my Bible or praying, but I just feel too depressed, and I am just not in the mood." Before you get angry with me, let me admit I've been there and have already expressed that I needed to be stripped of all but God to "wake up." Satan tries to trick us by getting us to think we need to set our minds on ourselves and our struggle before setting it on God. The truth is, setting your minds on God and off yourself is what is going to end up getting you to your breakthrough. The disciples made this mistake while they were in the boat with Jesus during a storm. Their minds were on themselves and the storm as they were just in a pure state of anxiety.

> Then He got into the boat and his disciples followed him. Suddenly a furious storm came up on the lake, so that the waves swept over the boat. But Jesus was sleeping. The disciples went and woke him, saying, "Lord save us! We are going to drown!" He replied, "You of little faith, why are you so afraid?" Then he got up and rebuked the

winds and the waves, and it was completely calm.
The men were amazed and asked, "What kind of
man is this? Even the winds and the waves obey
him!" (Matt. 8:23–27)

We see here that the disciples had their eyes on the big problem
they were facing rather than on Jesus, even while he was in the same
boat! I have to admit, I would have been freaking out in a threatening
storm, and I think I would have been waking Jesus up in a dramatic
fashion as well. I love that it says Jesus was sleeping, just like today
at times we question if God is listening to us. We want an immediate fix. I mean, who doesn't? Sometimes there is silence followed by
our prayers and it can be tiring when something isn't fixed when we
request it. The disciples wanted the storm to stop on their terms,
but Jesus calls them out by saying, "You of little faith, why are you
so afraid?" Basically, "Hey, disciples, I would have stopped it even if
you didn't alert me. Do you even remember who I am?" Even though
their faith was so miniscule, he still calmed the storm. Of course,
He is always listening and aware of it all, but He works in His own
perfect time. First Timothy 6:15 reads, "Which God will bring about
in his own time- God, the blessed and only Ruler, and the King of
kings and Lord of lords."

God is all-knowing and has mapped out every speck of your life
to flow into perfection even if it doesn't make sense to you right now.
Also, look at how many times, "Do not be afraid" is stated in the
Bible. It is all over the place! God was extra prepared when it came
to knowing how fear could encounter that individual by starting off
a conversation with, "Do not be afraid."

It should be our mission to get to our fortress, place our eyes
on God over our fear, anxiety, obsessive thinking, depression, etc. I
had to force myself at first to get into my new daily habits as my relationship with God grew by turning to Him over myself. When you
feel miserable, it's hard to take the focus off yourself because you are
subconsciously dwelling in this place of turmoil. I had mentioned I
moved home and made my mom sleep on the floor the first week out
of fear, but I still felt lonely. Everyone would go to work and I would

be stuck alone just saturated in this disgusting mind-set. I would call my mom, dad, and sister while they were at work just to have that temporary security on the other end. I would just repeat to them what they already had known, that I was obsessing over thoughts and they won't go away. It would help for the five minutes that I was on the phone, but it still was not enough long term. My eyes were continuing to look upon the storm, and giving it power was only making it intensify. Although it is a huge help to have people offer support and be there for you, it shouldn't be all you rely on. God first, then he will provide help through others for you. Forgive me for seeming like a broken record at times, but we are striving to create a new repetition in our lives, right? This is something we must make stick or we will easily drift back into our old harmful thinking patterns.

So we took a minor detour from our star Susie, but we didn't forget about her! The reason I brought up the story of the disciples and the storm is because this is Susie's present-day problem. We learned that she loves God but is choosing to dwell on her feelings rather than go to God. We need to get Susie to her fortress!

One morning, Susie is just so anxious that she feels out of control including every symptom of anxiety under the sun. She tries calling her family to try and find comfort, but unfortunately no one is available. Her anxiety increases as she is now panicking about being alone while this is happening. She walks into her kitchen, and her monthly calendar catches her eye. A beautiful picture of peaceful Smokey Mountains with a verse in bold black letters underneath, "The Lord will fight for you; you need only to be still" (Exod. 14:14). She is currently being anything but still. She is having sporadic panic attacks. Susie uncontrollably bursts into tears as she reads these words repeatedly and feels the presence of God for the first time in a while. The doubt in Susie's mind has just encountered an opponent that it doesn't recognize, and she is having an "oh yeah" moment. This verse alone has created such a craving for more that Susie decides to revisit it in her actual bible. Up until this valley of depression, Susie hasn't needed God to "fight for her," so this verse now has so much new meaning. The desperation for more of this promise drove Susie to look up more about God fighting for her, and to her surprise, it is said more than once:

> "Do not be afraid of them; the Lord your God himself will fight for you" (Deut. 3:22).

> "The Lord your God, who is going before you, will fight for you, as he did for you in Egypt, before your very eyes" (Deut. 1:30).

> "For the Lord your God is the one who goes *with you* to fight for you against your enemies to give you victory" (Deut. 20:4).

> "Wherever you hear the sound of the trumpet, join us there. Our God will fight for us!" (Neh. 4:20).

Susie has more than confirmed for herself that God is who she needs to be pursuing in order to enjoy her life. She realizes that she is calming down as her breathing is now slow and steady. She goes on with her day just hoping that is all she needed, but fear and anxiety push back and create a wall. This has been such a bad habit of Susie's that it is just naturally present in her mind. Remembering how she was able to make her anxiety dissipate earlier, Susie goes back to her Bible. She looks over the verses but goes a step further by writing them down and placing them on her fridge, mirror, and dashboard where she will constantly see them. What Susie may not realize is that she is slowly building up her strategic battle plan as she visits her fortress during times of struggle, all while keeping her armor on. It is becoming apparent that coming to God in desperation is all that is helping her climb out of her pit and she is craving it. Along with scripture and prayer, Susie begins to desire the offense over the defense as she strengthens in faith and strives for that loving relationship with God. She has never felt this close to God and He becomes just as important as her need to breathe. Susie develops an entirely different mind-set while in church and worships God with lyrics that match her heart. She is singing out to God with meaning and thankfulness with big tears in her eyes, tears of joy. Because she is starting to feel better, she starts her day early with a morning walk while listening to podcast sermons. Susie is even feeling good enough to wave to every passerby with a smile. She is no longer even tempted to lay in her bed emotionless and soaked in anxiety. God has shown her this whole new world and her tunnel centered on depression is breaking with glimpses of hope shining through. Susie develops a brand-new excitement for life! Now that she has matured in her faith, when anxiety enters her mind she remembers, "Be still," and enters her fortress. She has conquered depression and is able to make a decision with a clear mind and guidance from the Holy Spirit as she considers her future. She now leads a study at her church where she is able to use her testimony to help others. God has blessed her with an amazing gift of compassion for those in very dark places.

Susie's story is very similar to mine, other than the fancy doctor part (ha-ha). She was led by the Holy Spirit as she glanced at the scripture on her calendar, and that spark lit a bonfire of desire to pursue God in her time of need. She fought her "false evidence appearing real" with truth and ended up reaching her breakthrough. This is very possible for you as well, remember even Job made it! The society we live in today is just completely stress-filled. It's very hard not to worry. Those unknown futures, the haunting what-ifs.

So how can we be faced with fear and not worry about it? Jesus spoke of worry in Matthew 6:25:

> Therefore, I tell you, do not worry about your life, what you will eat or drink; or about your body, what you will wear. Is not life more than food, and the body more than clothes? Look at the birds of the air; they do not sow or reap or store away in barns, and yet your heavenly Father feeds them. Are you not much more valuable than they? Can any one of you by worrying add a single hour to your life? And why do you

worry about clothes? See how the flowers of the field grow. They do not labor or spin. Yet I tell you that not even Solomon in all his splendor was dressed like one of these. If that is how God clothes the grass of the field, which is here today and tomorrow is thrown into the fire, will he not much more clothe you- you of little faith? So do not worry, saying, 'What shall we eat?' or 'What shall we wear?' For the pagans run after all these things, and your heavenly Father knows that you need them. But seek first his kingdom and righteousness, and all these things will be given to you as well. Therefore, do not worry about tomorrow, for tomorrow will worry about itself. Each day has enough trouble of its own.

Again, just like the disciples in the boat, we are told here to keep our eyes off our worries, or our "storm." I remind myself of this verse sometimes when I see bird outside. I have yet to find a bird dwindling away due to starvation, and it resets my thinking immediately. My husband will say to me all of the time, "What good does it do worrying about it? Worrying will not change the outcome." I usually snarl at him because I know he is right, but don't worry—I hug him eventually out of love. This is what Jesus meant by saying, "Can any one of you by worrying add a single hour to your life?" What are you gaining by worrying yourself to the point of developing depression? Just like my example of not remembering the first year of my daughter's life, what did I gain from that? I tell you what, I didn't gain anything that I desired, and it was a waste of precious time. This isn't something to beat yourself up over, just something to pay close attention to. We will never stop having worrisome thoughts. It's just how you handle them that matters!

ATTACKING OBSESSIVE THINKING

I do not know the severity of your obsessive thinking, but if you are having symptoms of depression, I imagine you have at least experienced it. Obsessive thinking is a subcategory of anxiety but is enough of an issue to address. Scary thoughts are produced sometimes out of nowhere, and it is very confusing and frustrating when they do not make any sense. Your brain has been under so much stress and pressure to "fix" your current state that it is just handing you the most out-of-left-field thoughts possible. Satan considers himself successful when you begin the cycle of fear to anxiety, anxiety to obsessive scary thoughts, and scary thoughts to depression. Then the cycle just rotates these lovely phases as you allow yourself to be beaten to a pulp. Anxiety can provide spurts of panic that eventually lessen, while obsessive scary thoughts consume your thinking. You are so stuck on this thought that rational reasoning isn't even touching as you are trying to process it under anxious, unclear circumstances. The biggest lie from the devil is that these thoughts will never go away. I am here to tell you that they *do* go away and can be dealt with once and for all!

Just like I created a template for attacking anxiety, I am going to form one for obsessive thoughts, but this time in the form of questions. I have come up with four questions to ask yourself to cognitively think over when dissecting your thought. I know the type of thinker you are. You analyze and desire every ounce of evidence to give you peace.

1. Does this thought reflect my true identity?
2. Is it a rational thought?
3. What is said in the Word about this?
4. Will this thought ever go away?

Some of the answers to these are already addressed in the Word, but it helps to see in writing to better clarify for you. We anxiety sufferers like loads evidence to prove our fear to be false, thank goodness God and His word are rock solid! Since we have developed such a knack of analyzing everything in a negative way, why not use that skill in a positive way? In the beginning my fears were so scary that I eventually became solely fearful of the thoughts themselves, not just of them occurring. I learned that if I faced them and dissected them, the power of the thought would decrease. This has to be done at your own pace. There is no need to rush. Like I mentioned before with my representation of a turtle and myself. You can easily think you have conquered a thought, but it presents itself again with its threatening strength. That's okay, no need to get upset with yourself. You are in a renewal process and your mind is having to follow your new lead led by God. You are no longer allowing your mind to be Satan's garbage dump and it's going to take some time to break these strong and bad habits. If the bad thought pops up, just let it float in and float out to God. The thought itself cannot harm you, and He is willing to take it from you. To this day, I will even have an old thought pop up, one that used to cripple my mind in fear. I can feel its strength and deter-mination, but I fight back hard in my fortress. I will remind myself out loud, "I have already conquered this fear years ago by proving it to be invalid and harmless, and I will pass this test." My dad refers to these temporarily returning thoughts as "echoes." So I remind myself that it is just an echo, an attempt from Satan to push my buttons that were once very effective, and I move on. Most of the time I look back and laugh because it just shows how pathetic Satan can be. This level of thinking is attainable, and you can do it!

Now, I will go through the template based upon my past scary thought of "What if I go crazy?" I remember getting a postpartum depression book (which I never was clinically diagnosed, just worried about having. Surprise, surprise) and reading about "postpartum depression psychosis." Talk about "scary thought" land, oh my goodness! There were symptoms listed and one was "the feeling of bugs crawling on or under your skin." Guys, I literally was to the point where something would tickle my leg and I would panic with a sweat and think, "The psychosis is setting in!" I was allowing my mind to wander into making this scary thought valid based upon false evidence appearing real. Here is what my answers would have been:

1. *Does this thought reflect my true identity?* Well, mentally no, I am aware of my surroundings and can tell the difference between right and wrong. I have been told that people entering into a level of insanity do not even comprehend what is going on. I have seen crazy people before portrayed in movies and that is not how I am behaving. I am a child of God, and I am made in His image. My longing in life is to be Christ-like and Jesus knows right from wrong. If I am to live this way, I will continue to apply this Christ-likeness in my life and believe my mind will not be lost.

2. *Is it rational?* No, not at all. I have not been diagnosed with psychosis, nor has anyone been concerned that I may have it. (This question may be tricky for you because of the distortion caused by your overloaded brain. Again, it is trying to aid you by handing you something so scary that it confuses your view on it being rational or irrational.) To answer this question for myself, I would always pretend someone else had my exact scary thought and was coming to me about it. To my surprise, I viewed the thought completely irrational every time. This brought the thought into reality for a moment and made it seem so silly.

What is said in the Word about this? I would recall Philippians 2:5 (AMP): "For God did not give us a spirit of timidity or cowardice or fear, but [He has given us a spirit] of power and of love and of sound judgment and personal discipline abilities that result in a calm, well-balanced mind and self-control."

I have clarified that it is an irrational thought; therefore God has given me a spirit of a calm, well-balanced mind and self-control. This is the opposite of insanity, and I can breathe a sigh of relief!

Will this thought ever go away? Yes, they do go away and will not last forever. I would then remind myself of the scary thoughts I had gotten over in the past to prove that they no longer bothered me. Most of the time I laugh at how silly they sound, even though at the time they were anything but silly. Just like the phrase, "This too shall pass," you will eventually move on as you gain strength in that area. Here is your biblical confirmation in this:"Nevertheless, that time of darkness and despair will not go on forever" (Isa. 9:1).

Nothing is more frustrating than a scary thought just hounding you for more of your attention and stealing your present moment. I always tried to envision myself stepping above a scary thought, putting it in its place. Doing so made me visualize that I have control over it. Get above it, get on the offense. It is your call on how much you will let these thoughts bully you, evict them from your mind just like a splinter out of your skin. They have no place there, and God did not create you to cower to them. Something I always say out loud to God is, "Let my thoughts match your thoughts. Let my heart match your heart."

"A calm and undisturbed mind and heart
are the life and health of the body" (Prov. 14:30).

If we are to model ourselves after Jesus Christ, that means matching all of him to the best of our ability. Now, obviously God's mind will always exceed mine in understanding and wisdom, but I am talking about in our situations. How would his thoughts sound?

"Therefore, holy brothers and sister, who
share in the heavenly calling, fix your thoughts
on Jesus, whom we acknowledge as our apostle
and high priest" (Heb. 3:1).

My daughter got one of those "best friends" necklaces that contains two pieces of a heart that attach with magnets. I was the lucky one to get the other half, but I would forget to wear it and she would get pretty upset with me. She loved joining them while they were still on our necks. I think it just simply made her feel connected with me. This was not an easy task as we stretched our necks awkwardly to connect, but we would get them to match and it reminded me of what I pray. Sometimes we have to take a step back and literally think, "What would be going through Jesus's mind during this, and how would his mind and heart react?"

The template I created for you is based upon a thought that is irrational, but what about when the answer could be, "Yes, this is a rational thought?" Well, just because it's rational does not mean that it is going to happen. Let's take for example my earlier story of the birth of my fear of getting sick. We could say that was a rational fear considering I had eaten the same sausage patty my sister did that gave her food poisoning, but that still isn't enough to be certain it will happen. Scary thoughts can also be formed around something that you know for sure is going to happen in the future, like surgery. Say you are going to get your wisdom teeth extracted and you are allowing the anticipation and unknown eat you alive. This is something that is set in stone to happen and you unfortunately cannot avoid it. In reality though, "What does God say about this?" could silence your thought because He alone gives us peace. That question gets your wheels turning and your feet running to your fortress, and the other questions don't even matter anymore. You are in that fortress with full protection from God. Those walls are rock solid. Nothing can touch you. You no longer need explanation or a dissection of your thought. You casted your care and He has you. But like I have said many times, this is a practice you need to learn and mature into. I know this part is so hard and tiring. I look back and sometimes cannot believe I made it out of that pit, but I did. You will get there. Just hold on. You've got this!

ATTACKING DEPRESSION

So do not fear, for I am with you; do not be dismayed, for I am your God. I will strengthen you and help you; I will uphold you with my righteous right hand.

—Isaiah 41:10

Ah, depression, the unfortunate result of endless fear, anxiety, and obsessive thinking swirling around in our head and not being disposed of correctly. I think it's safe to say that depression is a very common condition, and you will find more people struggle with it than you knew. It's frowned upon in our society and may be responsible for people being labeled "weak" because of this. In a way, we are weak on our own, but not with God:

> But he said to me, "My grace is sufficient for you, for my power is made perfect in weakness." Therefore, I will boast all the more gladly about my weaknesses, so that Christ's power may rest on me. That is why, for Christ's sake, I delight in weaknesses, in insults, in hardships, in persecutions, in difficulties. For when I am weak, then I am strong. (2 Cor. 12:9–11)

This onset of new awful feelings can make anyone retract despite their life prior. You are saturated, weighed down and are in this hopeless mind-set and you need the key to unlock the door. The good news is that if you practice working on your fears, anxiety, and obsessive thinking, the depression will make its grand exit. Because of these negative influences, your brain just enters into this state of overload and is tired of processing everything to make sense. We can create a positive domino effect as we knock each bad influence out in order to reach our breakthrough with God by our side. Sometimes we feel stuck here, like we will never shake this new way of living and we must learn to just cope with it. I know when I had all the tools ready and was doing everything I was advised to do. I still felt like I was going nowhere for a bit.

I used to have this old 1974 Piaggio Vespa moped when I was about ten years old. I saved up all of my allowance to buy this thing and ride it all over the neighborhood in order to look cool. This moped was a beast and was basically a big tetanus shot waiting to happen. The catch was that you had to pedal it on the kickstand while holding the clutch and pulling the throttle back. I cannot tell you how many times I pedaled so much that I broke a sweat and gave myself a good thigh work out without it even showing signs of it starting. The wheels were turning at a rapid speed, but I was going nowhere. I would get so frustrated that I would jump off and maybe kick the tire or scream at it. I actually have a scar on my finger from the clutch, so I will never forget my beautiful piece-of-junk moped. Anyway, this is us—we commit to freeing ourselves of this depression, and nothing! How, and why is this happening if we are doing everything we can to better our life? The best biblical example I can compare this dilemma to, is the Israelites in the wilderness. I am so thankful for this example in the Bible, because it helped me immensely out of my pit. We are going to have a lot of scripture to go through here, and it may seem tedious, but a bunch of light bulbs are about to go off in your mind so hang tight!

THE WILDERNESS

*M*erriam-*Webster* defines *wilderness* as "a tract or region uncultivated and uninhabited by human beings, essentially undisturbed by human activity with its naturally developed life community, and an empty or pathless area of region." Sounds a lot like a metaphor of our mind during depression. It's pretty much inhabitable in there. Seriously picture yourself in an actual setting of the wilderness somewhere off the grid. There are probably overgrown vines, bushes, trees, and weeds doing whatever they please without rules. The bugs are just out of control and swarm around you looking for something to nag and bite. I don't even want to know the chances of coming across a snake or a spider as big as your face are. The smell is musty, full of humidity and mildew, and you have nowhere to escape. Threatening animals are present and are considering you prey as they lurk and stalk you. This is definitely not a desirable place to hang out long term, maybe on a one-day excursion with a tour guide, protective gear and a trustworthy vehicle.

My mind was not a pleasant place to visit during my depression, and like I have mentioned before, we cannot run from our own mind. We are stuck in the wilderness, and we can prolong our stay if we are not careful enough. You wouldn't choose to physically stay in a wilderness for longer than your comfort allowed, so why stay there in your mind? The Israelites spent some time in the wilderness after leaving Egypt where they were heavily mistreated. I'm going to storytell with scripture, while making some points for you personally along the way. I could paraphrase this all day, but I want you to feel it by reading it yourself. There is nothing like reading the actual scripture, and seeing the truth firsthand rather than it being spoon fed to you through someone else's choice words. Let's check out the history of the Israelites:

> So they put slave masters over them to oppress them with forced labor, and they built Pithom and Rameses as store cities for Pharaoh. But the more they were oppressed, the more they multiplied and spread; so the Egyptians came to dread the Israelites and worked them ruthlessly. They made their lives bitter with harsh labor in brick and mortar and with all kinds of work in the fields; in all their harsh labor the Egyptians worked them ruthlessly.(Exod. 1:11–14)

You see here that the point is made twice to signify how poorly they were treated, "worked them ruthlessly." They needed a big change in life. They were heavily mistreated slaves. This change definitely wasn't projected to be easy, but God was at work and had a plan with a leader in mind:

> Now a man of the tribe of Levi married a Levite woman, and she became pregnant and gave birth to a son. When she saw that he was a fine child, she hid him for three months. But when she could hide him no longer, she got a papyrus basket for him and coated it with tar and pitch. Then she placed the child in it and put it among the reeds along the bank of the Nile. His sister stood at a distance to see what would happen to him. Then Pharaoh's daughter went down to the Nile to bathe, and her attendants were walking along the riverbank. She saw the basket among the reeds and sent her female slave to get it. She opened it and saw the baby. He was crying, and she felt sorry for him. "This is one of the Hebrew babies," she said. Then his sister asked Pharaoh's

daughter, "Shall I go and get one of the Hebrew women to nurse the baby for you?" "Yes go," she answered. So, the girl went and got the baby's mother. Pharaoh's daughter said to her, "Take this baby and nurse him for me, and I will pay you." So, the woman took the baby and nursed him. When the child grew older, she took him to Pharaoh's daughter and he became her son. She named him Moses, saying, "I drew him out of the water.(Exod. 2:1–10)

How incredible is this plan of God's? It is amazing to me how he takes dire situations and works to orchestrate His will. The reason Moses's mother did this was because Pharaoh gave order to throw every Hebrew boy that is born into the Nile but allow the girls to live. Obviously, Satan was behind the fact that the baby boys were to be thrown into the river, but God turned this evil plan into good by getting Moses into a position where he was able to someday help his people. He needed a leader who was strong and able to withstand what he was about to endure:

One day, after Moses had grown up, he went out to where his own people were and watched them at their hard labor. He saw an Egyptian beating a Hebrew, one of his own people. Looking this way and that and seeing no one, he killed the Egyptian and hid him in the sand. The next day he went out and saw two Hebrews fighting. He asked the one in the wrong, "Why are you hitting your fellow Hebrew?" The man said, "Who made you ruler and judge over us? Are you thinking of killing me as you killed the Egyptian?" Then Moses was afraid and thought, "What I did must have become known." When Pharaoh heard of this, he tried to kill Moses, but Moses fled from

Pharaoh and went to live in Midian, where he sat
down by a well.(Exod. 2:11–15)

God is preparing Moses for his position to lead the Israelites
out of Egypt as he is bothered by the treatment of his people and
decides to step in and do something about it. This now makes him
an enemy of those who raised him, and he flees to avoid being killed.
To me, this represents leaving our old mind-set and ways of life and
preparing to journey to our new God-ordained life. Ephesians 4:20-
24 explains this process so well:

> That however, is not the way of life you
> learned when you heard about Christ and were
> taught in him in accordance with the truth that
> is in Jesus. You were taught, with regard to your
> former way of life, to put off your old self, which
> is being corrupted by its deceitful desires; to be
> made new in the attitude of your minds; and to
> put on the new self, created to be like God in true
> righteousness and holiness.

Before my onset, I was nowhere near the model of Jesus Christ
that I could be, and I was strongly lacking my relationship with
God. I thought all was good, but I was self-centered and I needed
a drastic change. Moses has a sheer panic moment after he kills the
Egyptian for beating the Hebrew, and he knows there are changes on
the way. He was living a life representing the very people that were
abusing those he came from. Moses's transition to being a leader of
the Israelites starts to take place where he lands in Midian:

> Now a priest of Midian had seven daughters,
> and they came to draw water and fill the troughs
> to water their father's flock. Some shepherds came
> along and drove them away, but Moses got up
> and came to their rescue and watered their flock.
> When the girls returned to Reuel their father, he

asked them, "Why have you returned so early today?" They answered, "An Egyptian rescued us from the shepherds. He even drew water for us and watered the flock." (Eph. 2:16)

Reuel is so impressed that he ends up giving his daughter Zipporah to Moses in marriage. A long time goes by, signifying that the Israelites are waiting incredibly long for change in their life. The king of Egypt dies, but still there are no changes in the treatment of the Israelites:"The Israelites groaned in their slavery and cried out, and their cry for help because of their slavery went up to God. God heard their groaning and he remembered his covenant with Abraham, with Isaac, and with Jacob. So God looked on the Israelites and was concerned about them" (Exod. 2:23–25)

Merriam-Webster defines *covenant* as "a written agreement or promise usually under seal between two or more parties especially for the performance of some action." This is so awesome, because it is showing us that God hears us and keeps His promises. God hearing prayers and pleas for help is all over the Bible:

"Hear my prayer, Lord; listen to my cry for mercy" (Ps. 86:6).

"Then from heaven, your dwelling place, hear their prayer and their plea, and uphold their cause" (1 Kings 8:49).

"Answer me when I call to you, my righteous God. Give me relief from my distress; have mercy on me and hear my prayer" (Ps. 4:1).

"But as for me, I watch in hope for the Lord, I wait for God my Savior; my God will hear me" (Micah 7:7).

"Then he continued, 'Do not be afraid Daniel. Since the first day that you set your mind to gain understanding and to humble yourself before your God, your words were heard, and I have come in response to them'" (Dan. 10:12).

"The righteous cry out, and the Lord hears them; he delivers them from all their troubles" (Ps. 34:17).

"Therefore I tell you, whatever you ask for in prayer, believe that you have received it, and it will be yours" (Mark 11:24).

I think this may be enough to show that prayer is heard by God, but again, we anxious and depressed folks need proof, so I went overboard for you. I have heard so many times the phrase *the power of prayer*. I thought this was just a little pick-me-up for the majority of my life, but after looking through verses on God hearing our cry for help through prayer, it suddenly shows its power. Moses is encountered by God through a burning bush here in Exodus 3:4–10:

When the Lord saw that he had gone over to look, God called to him from within the bush, "Moses! Moses!" And Moses said, "Here I am." "Do not come any closer, God said. "Take off your sandals, for the place where you are standing is holy ground." Then he said, "I am the God of your father, the God of Abraham, the God of Isaac, and the God of Jacob." At this, Moses hid his face, because he was afraid to look at God. The Lord said, "I have indeed seen the misery of my people in Egypt. I have heard them crying out because of their slave drivers, and I am concerned about their suffering. So, I have come down to rescue them from the hand of the Egyptians and to bring them up out of that land into a good and spacious land, a land flowing with milk and honey- the home of the Canaanites, Hittites, Amorites, Perizzites, Hivites and Jebusites. And now the cry of the Israelites has reached me, and I have seen the way the Egyptians are oppressing them. So now, go, I am sending you to Pharaoh to bring my people the Israelites out of Egypt.

A lot of things parallel with our journey out of depression in these verses. It would have been so amazing during my depression if I was sought out by God through a bush telling me that He saw me in my misery, was concerned, and He had a plan that was sure to get me out. Don't you just want that certainty out of His mouth directly? Don't worry, you already have it, if you have faith and trust in God. In this story, the Egyptians represent Satan against our mind. "So I have come down to rescue them from the hand of the Egyptians and to bring them up out of the land into a good spacious land, a land flowing with milk and honey." God doesn't just want to get the Israelites away from the Egyptians, He wants to bless them with a paradise to live in. Just like Job, for all of his terrible turmoil, God blessed him twice as much for remaining faithful and pursuing Him. This wasn't just going to be a snap of God's fingers and the job was done. There was some work to be done physically, emotionally, spiritually, and mentally on everyone's part.

But Moses said to God, "Who am I that I should go to Pharaoh to bring my people, the Israelites out of Egypt? And God said, "I will be with you. And this will be the sign to you that it is I who have sent you: When you have brought the people out of Egypt, you will worship God on this mountain. Moses said to God, "Suppose I go to the Israelites and say to them, 'The God of your father has sent me to you,' and they ask me, 'What is his name? Then what shall I tell them?" God said to Moses, "I AM WHO I AM. This is what you are to say to the Israelites: 'I AM sent me to you." God also said to Moses, "Say to the Israelites, 'The Lord, the God of your fathers-the God of Abraham, the God of Isaac and the God of Jacob has sent me to you.' "This is my name forever, the name you shall call me from generation to generation. Go, assemble the elders of Israel and say to them, 'The Lord, the God of your fathers—the God of Abraham, Isaac and Jacob—appeared to me and said: I have watched over you and have seen what has been done to you in Egypt. And I have promised to bring you up out of your misery in Egypt into the land of the Canaanites, Hittites, Amorites, Perizzites Hivites and Jebusites—a land flowing with milk and honey.'(Exod. 3:11–17)

I love this interaction between Moses and God, especially since I have many similarities in anxiety. They dance back and forth as Moses fears his calling and his what-ifs are flowing out of his mouth as he pictures himself failing already. Just like my doubts in writing this book, it was tempting to say, "God, honestly, I am no fit for this, pick someone else." You can tell God was getting a little stern toward Moses when it came to his doubt. With each response, He adds more power and authority in His answer with caps lock in text. "I AM WHO I AM!" This reminds me so much of "IT IS WRITTEN," and "You of little faith why did you doubt?" But we are all guilty of doubt at times, even when God speaks to us through a burning bush or in a storm with Jesus next to us in a boat. In case you may not have noticed by now, God doesn't call the qualified. He qualifies the called. Right now He is qualifying you to be a conqueror of depression:"No, in all these things we are more than conquerors through him who loved us" (Rom. 8:37).

This is one of my favorite verses to say out loud during an attack on my mind, "I am more than a conqueror!" *Merriam-Webster* defines *conqueror* as "to gain mastery over or win by overcoming obstacles or opposition." Being a conqueror would be enough of a gift from God, but we are even more than this! It's even hard for me to fathom what more than a conqueror would look like. I was a very shy and reserved child. Even into my adulthood, I was a follower, not a leader. I would have rather listened than be heard, and I avoided conflict at all costs. You can imagine the moment I realized God was calling me to be the one to fight alongside Him in my tiresome battle of depression. "Can't someone else fight for me? God, you out of everyone should know this does not align with my personality!" This was God's response as I read through scripture: "You of little faith why did you doubt. I AM WHO I SAY I AM. IT IS WRITTEN!"

Moses continues to doubt with more what-ifs in Exodus 4:1–13 (emphasis added):

> Moses answered, "What if they do not believe me or listen to me and say, 'The Lord did not appear to you'?" Then the Lord said to him, "What is that in your hand?" "A staff," he replied. The Lord said, "Throw it on the ground." Moses threw it on the ground and it became a snake, and he ran from it. Then the Lord said to him, "Reach out your hand and take it by the tail." So Moses reached out and took hold of the snake and it turned back into a staff in his hand. "This," said the Lord, "Is so that they may believe that the Lord, the God of their fathers—the God of Abraham, the God of Isaac and the God of Jacob—has appeared to you. Then the Lord said, "Put your hand inside your cloak." So Moses put his hand into his cloak, and when he took it out, the skin was leprous—it had become as white as snow. Now put it back into your cloak, and when he took it out, it was restored, like the rest of his flesh…Moses said to the Lord, "Pardon your servant, Lord. I have never been eloquent, neither

in the past nor since you have spoken to your servant. I am slow to speech and tongue." The Lord said to him," Who gave human beings their mouths? Who makes them deaf or mute? Who gives them sight or makes them blind? Is it not I the Lord? Now go; I will help you speak and will teach you what to say." But Moses said, "Pardon your servant, Lord. *Please send someone else.*"

Moses is coming up with every excuse in the book not to do what God is asking him to as fear is overcoming him. I don't think he's lazy or careless, I honestly think he does not see himself fit. Can you imagine going against those who raised you after you ticked them off, all while bringing the people that keep their land running away from them? We continue this back and forth with our doubt and then reassurance from God. We keep touching our fortress wall from the outside, but not stepping fully in enough to make our fear vanish. God is simply asking for Moses's trust all around, every inch of him needs to trust God, and Moses is not quite there yet.

To gain Moses's trust, God ends up having to bust out the spiritual physical proof as He turns Moses's staff into a snake and then changes the condition of his very own skin. By now Moses believes God is almighty and powerful, but it's taking him a bit to understand that God will give him strength and He will equip him for this intimidating task. Once you enter your fortress and are above your fear, that peace will just carry through with you.

I will never forget the time my husband called me to tell he had to come home to pack a bag as his ship was heading out because of a hurricane approaching. Apparently, the ship is safer out at sea rather than against a dock. I stared at my four-month-old daughter playing on the floor as he told me this news. I am from Michigan, where hurricanes are never present. I am not fit for this task. Thoughts immediately made their way into my mind and my head was spinning, especially the comment I heard the day prior: "This area was formed from a hurricane long ago." Oh, how lovely, if one is able to actually form a livable place for people to live on, what can it do to an already existing one? At the time, we also had three cats we were responsible for. Yes, you read that right, three. People were planning on evacuating as they were predicting the storm to impact hard. Chris came home and started throwing stuff in bags as I followed him like a little lost puppy. "What am I going to do!" "What am I going to do?" I did not have the heart to leave the cats abandoned. I had no idea how long I would be gone. This was serious and I was being called to journey alone, with a baby, and three cats. My husband is very observant and compassionate toward my anxiety, but he ended up getting pretty stern and honest as he looked at me and said, "You are going to have to figure it out calmly." He was right. What choice did I have? I started packing for our trip, kissed him goodbye, put the baby and our cats in the SUV, and headed north to home. I remember exactly when my panic and fear ceased, and I entered my fortress. I was about to get money out of the ATM for the trip, and every single cat tried to get out with me like we were escaping a clown car. I hadn't even left yet! I took a deep breath, looked at my beautiful daughter, and remembered whose child I was, and that he would provide strength in my huge weakness. I had to get above my fears and protect my daughter and myself.

I hit some big obstacles on this eleven-hour trip alone. I won't lie. One cat literally rolled the window down with his own paw, then jumped out of the window as I grabbed his leg. Another cat jumped onto my baby's car seat and scratched her little face while trying to stabilize himself. I nursed against a steering wheel and changed the baby's diaper on a Burger King booth because they had no changing table. Also, my GPS thought it would be fun to take me backway home through narrow roads on steep mountains in the dark. But, guys, I made it. I had such a peace from God that helped me push through. He was with me every millisecond of the way. This trip was one of the many pillars I gained in strength and endurance that contributes to me still today. I now look back and laugh at how crazy of a time it was, but honestly it is something I am very proud of. I also have such a special bond with my daughter because of times like these, and I am ever so grateful for that. Some of the situations I have found myself in are definitely not built for anxious people, but that is the point. If God brings you to it, He will bring you through it!

Moses ends up meeting up with his brother Aaron and tells him everything the Lord had told him:"Moses and Aaron brought together all the elders of the Israelites, and Aaron told them everything the Lord had said to Moses. He also performed the signs before the people, and they believed. And when they heard the Lord was concerned about them and had seen their misery they bowed down and worshipped" (Exod. 4:29–31).

So, from witnessing these signs you'd think that the Israelites would just have a never-ending trust in God. I am going to be honest. The Israelites are about to enter some physical, spiritual, emotional, and mental attacks from the enemy. I am sure there is a lot going through their minds. They are most likely hoping for a quick and smooth transition to paradise. Just like how we raise our kids, what good does it do them to do everything for them when they eventually need to learn how to be independent adults someday? I wish I had just fully trusted God the minute I had my panic attack that led into depression. Wouldn't we love for God to just bring his hand down on us and "poof" we are healed instantly? I will tell you this. I am now so grateful that this wasn't the case, because I would not be who I am today if He didn't allow me to go through it.

Like I said before, we are relating the Egyptians to Satan's attack on our minds, as he is going to push harder and harder each time you reach a breakthrough. The day comes when Moses and Aaron are to command Pharaoh to release the Israelites:"Afterward Moses and Aaron went to Pharaoh and said, 'This is what the Lord, the God of Israel, says: "Let my people go, so that they may hold a festival to me in the wilderness"'" (Exod. 5:1).

Pharaoh and the Egyptians claim full ownership of the Israelites and feel that it is their choice what is done with them because of this. But God claims the Israelites as His and He is demanding their release from this torturous life. God also claims you as his child, but Satan is fighting for custody rights. You have been dwelling in Satan's masterpiece, and while you aren't "possessed" by Satan, your mind is still falling for his tricks. Because you have been allowing this for so long, he knows your weaknesses and he is more than willing to use them against you to create opposition. Pharaoh basically thinks that Moses and Aaron are bluffing and shows irritation as they are creating a kink in their workday. He tells them that he will definitely not let them go and thinks they are pretty out of line for claiming a God unknown to him would command this to happen. Pharaoh doesn't go down without a fight. He turns up the heat:

> That same day Pharaoh gave this order to the slave drivers and overseers in charge of the people: "You are no longer to supply the people with straw for making bricks; let them go and gather their own straw. But require them to make the same number of bricks as before; don't reduce the quota. They are lazy; that is why they are crying out, 'Let us go and sacrifice to our God.' Make the work harder for the people so that they keep working and pay no attention to lies.(Exod. 5:6–9)

I think it is humorous that Pharaoh believes the Israelites are being lied to. He is the one being lied to by Satan, as he thinks allowing turmoil on the Israelites is morally okay. Jesus calls Satan a liar in John 8:44: "You belong to your father, the devil, and want to carry out your father's desires. He was a murderer from the beginning, not holding to the truth, for there is no truth in him. When he lies, he speaks his native language, for he is a liar and *father of lies*."

"Father of lies" is something I will say out loud during an attack I may be having to remind myself that I am not to believe Satan's deceit. I will even direct it toward Satan himself. Put him in his place! "You are the father of all lies and I am not going to fall for your traps!" Remember, anything that is not in agreement with God's Word is not from God, it is from Satan. The Israelite's job gets even harder as the condition of Pharaoh's heart is shown by worsening their work load. He's not going to meet the request of Moses and Aaron, and he is going to "show them!" This is seriously such a good match to a movie villain, how cruel. Let's check out how the Israelites react to this new order:

> Then the slave drivers and the overseers went out and said to the people, "This is what Pharaoh says: 'I will not give you any more straw wherever you can find it, but your work will not be reduced at all.'" So the people scattered all over Egypt to gather stubble to use for straw. The slave drivers kept pressing them, saying, "Complete the work required of you for each day, just as when you had straw." And Pharaoh's slave drivers beat the Israelite overseers they had appointed, demanding, "Why haven't you met your quota of bricks yesterday, as before?" Then the Israelite overseers went and appealed to Pharaoh: "Why have you treated your servants this way? Your servants are given no straw, yet we are told, 'Make bricks!' Your servants are being beaten, but the fault is with your own people. Pharaoh said, "Lazy, that's what you are- lazy! That is why you keep saying, 'Let us go and sacrifice to the Lord.' Now get to work. You will not be given any straw, yet you must produce your full quota of bricks." The Israelite overseers realized they were in trouble when they were told, "You are not to reduce the number of bricks required of you each day." When they left Pharaoh, they found Moses and Aaron waiting to meet them, and they said, "May the Lord look on you and judge you! You have made us obnoxious to Pharaoh and his officials and have put a sword in their hand to kill us." (Exod. 5:10–20)

I have never been a slave making bricks, but I can imagine its very dirty, tough, and tiring work. I am sure there are a lot of heavy things to carry all while sweating and being whipped by slave drivers to perform adequately. The command to make things even harder by taking away the resource used to make the bricks and not changing the quota sounds impossible. Then Pharaoh blames what the Israelites claim to be impossible on their laziness. This is such a terrible psychological lie. Just like Satan tries to trick us into thinking something is wrong with us for the way we are feeling, when it is his doing. Pharaoh himself made a request that was impossible to complete, so he made up an excuse why it wasn't being accomplished. This is the first opposition the Israelites face after they have been told they will be saved. Again, I think they were hoping for an immediate release, so they are confused. They approach Moses and Aaron telling them that they made things worse for them and are now paying the price. This is us in our depression when we realize there is some work and refinement to be done before our breakthrough. We get cold feet as we face opposition from the devil in our journey and start questioning our capability. Satan flings lies at us so hard during this time because he knows the authority you possess, and his biggest fear is you discovering it. These lies may sound like this, "This is impossible because I am not strong enough, and I do not have it in me to fight." Just like Pharaoh's made-up excuses of laziness, Satan will give you excuses to believe about yourself. Moses was confused by this hurdle in Exodus 5:22–23, 6:1–8:

> Moses returned to the Lord and said, "Why, Lord, why have you brought trouble on this people? Is this why you sent me? Ever since I went to Pharaoh to speak in your name, he brought trouble on this people, and you have not rescued your people at all." Then the Lord said to Moses, "Now you will see what I will do to Pharaoh: Because of my mighty hand he will let them go; because of my mighty hand he will drive them out of his country." God also said to Moses, "I am the Lord. I appeared to Abraham, to Isaac and to Jacob as God almighty, but by my name

the Lord I did not make myself fully known to
them. I also established my covenant with them
to give them the land of Canaan, where they
resided as foreigners. Moreover, I have heard the
groaning of the Israelites, whom the Egyptians
are enslaving, and I have remembered my covenant. "Therefore, say to the Israelites: 'I am the
Lord, and I will bring you out from under the
yoke of the Egyptians. I will free you from being
slaves to them, and I will redeem you with an
outstretched arm and with mighty acts of judgement. I will take you as my own people, and I
will be your God. Then you will know that I am
the Lord your God, who brought you out from
under the yoke of the Egyptians. And I will bring
you to the land I swore with uplifted hand to give
to Abraham, to Isaac and to Jacob. I will give it to
you as a possession, I am Lord.'"

I think the flesh in me would have questioned the situation. I
know it did during my own personal depression. "I thought you were
going to rescue me. Why is this still going on? Why do I feel worse
than I did before I accepted your help God?" Just like my moped,
I was pedaling to start it, but I was going nowhere. However, there
were times I would find strength and I would pedal faster and it
would start up, because I kept pressing on.

I have been told by people I help coach out of depression, "I
don't recognize who I am anymore. I don't know what my identity is." It is truly frightening when you notice that you are not the
same. First of all, it is a good thing you do not recognize who you
are because you are in the process of being refined, and God is our
Refiner.

"See, I have refined you, though not as sil-
ver; I have tested you in the furnace of affliction"
(Isa. 48:10).

> "I will refine them like silver and test them like gold. They will call on my name and I will answer them; I will say, 'They are my people,' and they will say, 'The Lord is our God'" (Zech. 13:9).

> Seems like a big job to be refined. How do we know which way we are to be molded in God's will? God's got that part covered: "Yet you, Lord, are our Father. We are the clay, you are the potter; we are all the work of your hand" (Isa. 64:8).

Obviously if you are brought to this journey by God, some changes in your life are needed, but God is going to help mold you. Secondly, our identity is in Christ as children of God, then our interests on earth fall into place. In college I was caught in the wrong crowd, listened to music that was badly influential, had a mouth like a sailor, gossiped about others, and didn't have my ongoing relationship with God. That identity was slowly slipping away, and it was scary because that was where I sat in comfort for so long. But God wasn't comfortable with it, and I needed to be shown I shouldn't be either.

The Israelites at this point are reaching new levels of refinement as conditions are worsening and they are now wishing they just had stayed the way they were. "Ugh, why did you interfere, Moses? This is not worth it?" What I didn't see during this refinement process of myself is the outcome, the new me.

> "Therefore, if anyone is in Christ, the new creation has come: The old has gone, the new is here!" (2 Cor. 2:17).

The Israelites are just getting their first glimpse of the trials they are about to face, and they are already retracting. God was prepared ahead of time for this opposition as he said to Moses:"Now you will see what I will do to Pharaoh: Because of my mighty hand he will let them go; because of my mighty hand he will drive them out of his country" (Exod. 6:1).

God goes on to remind Moses of his power and authority and that he has heard the groans of the Israelites and that he has remembered His covenant. Then he instructs Moses:

> Therefore, say to the Israelites: "I am the Lord, and I will bring you out from under the yoke of the Egyptians. I will free you from being slaves to them, and I will redeem you with an outstretched arm and with mighty acts of judgement. I will take you as my own people, and I will be your God. Then you will know that I am the Lord your God, who brought you out from under the yoke of the Egyptians. And I will bring you to the land I swore with uplifted hand to give to Abraham, to Isaac and to Jacob. I will give it to you as a possession. I am the Lord. Moses reported this to the Israelites, but they did not listen to him because of their discouragement and harsh labor. Then the Lord said to Moses, "Go tell Pharaoh King of Egypt to let the Israelites go out of his country." But Moses said to the Lord, "If the Israelites will not listen to me, why would Pharaoh listen to me, since I speak with faltering lips?" (Exod. 6:6–12)

How familiar does this sound, this back and forth? The Israelites had direct word from God spoken through Moses and Aaron that God saw them and would rescue them. After their first setback, they are frustrated and discouraged and no longer believe this is going to happen. We have direct confirmation from God in the Word full of God's love, faith, promises, guidance, grace, mercy, etc. We also have Godly people around us that will speak in our pain what God has put directly on their heart for us. You will know when this happens as you will think, "That can only be God!"

God continues to reference what He gave Abraham, Isaac, and Jacob, and that He will keep His covenant with them as well. This also reminds me of the process of renewing your mind. God keeps repeating himself in order to form a habitual thinking pattern in the Israelites' minds. Just like parents sometimes have to remind their children of their authority. I do it all of the time, "You are the child, and mommy and daddy are the adults in charge of everything." Obviously, this doesn't always stick as they need reminders constantly, but eventually as they age and mature, they will know who call the shots until they are legally adults. This is also another time Moses questions his ability to follow through with orders, "If the Israelites will not listen to me, why would Pharaoh listen to me, since I speak with faltering lips?" If the very people he is trying to free won't listen, then why would the very people in charge of their slavery listen?

God then commands Moses and Aaron to bring the Israelites out of Egypt and Moses again repeats his concern: "Since I speak with faltering lips, why would Pharaoh listen to me?" (Exod. 6:30).

I would be a hypocrite by saying I would like to slap Moses, so I won't say it. I too have had things said to me repeatedly many times before finally believing them. When I am coaching people, the hardest part is getting them over that first hurdle of doubt once they enter their journey toward breakthrough. Not only are you looking out for them to get over this hurdle, Satan is very aware of it, as he created it. We have such a distorted mind-set that we need clarity in knowing to expect that as we progress things will come against us. If you feel this opposition while following God, you my friend are doing it right. Why would Satan cause opposition if you were no threat to him? Expect it, and keep going on. Check out what happens next:

> Then the Lord said to Moses, "See, I have made you like God to Pharaoh, and your brother Aaron will be your prophet. You are to say everything I command you, and your brother Aaron is to tell Pharaoh to let the Israelites go out of his country. But I will harden Pharaoh's heart,

and though I multiply my signs and wonders in Egypt, he will not listen to you. Then I will lay my hand on Egypt and with mighty acts of judgement I will bring out my divisions, my people the Israelites. And the Egyptians will know that I am the Lord when I stretch out my hand against Egypt and bring the Israelites out of it." (Exod. 7:1–5)

Satan's goal is enslavement of God's children, just like Pharaoh claims ownership of the Israelites. We have been slaves to the mind-sets Satan has tricked us into developing, and God wants to free you of this. God is preparing Moses for Pharaoh's reaction and denial in the request to free the Israelites. Satan is obviously the same as he works overtime to oppose our progress. But, just like we have learned already, we have authority over him! Can you imagine if we had to ask permission to be free from him? Thank you, Jesus, for paying that price for us! God decides that it's time for him to step in and fight for his people by stretching his hand against Egypt and bringing the Israelites out of it! God is basically saying, "Enough is enough. I am here for you my children."

I have been trying my hardest to teach my children confidence and to lovingly stand up for themselves, but sometimes there is need for interference. I remember a play date I took my daughter on when she was about two years old. This little girl kept taking every single toy my daughter would pick up, and she was pushing her down relentlessly. I kept looking at the mother waiting for her to say something as I was also paying attention to my daughter's reaction. I always try to let them work it out, but in this situation, my daughter had taken enough and was in need of her mother. I ended up telling the little girl, "No, thank you," but we politely ended up leaving because it continued without the mother trying to help. Definitely a way different scale than the Israelites, but same concept. I heard my daughter's plea to be rescued and when the child's mother would not cooperate with disciplining her daughter, I "fought" for my child. But even though I fought for her, as she ages, I expect her to learn how to defend herself against those that come against her. God expects the same of us as we are to protect ourselves against Satan's schemes. Here with the Israelites, God is planning on stepping in on their "play date" and defending His children but with the expectation that they continuously follow his guidance along the way. Just because He is rescuing them, doesn't mean Satan will leave them alone. There is a renewal process for them as well, and a relationship desired centered on trust.

I am going to share a lot of actual text I want to sum up. I definitely encourage you to check out the detail within those chapters when you get a chance. For now, I am simply pointing out the huge impact God has on this situation in bits and pieces of verses.

Moses and Aaron begin to perform amazing miracles in front of Pharaoh, but his heart hardens just like God said it would, and he still doesn't listen to them. In order to get Pharaoh's attention, God brings down ten plagues upon Egypt including the plague of blood, frogs, gnats, flies, livestock, boils, hail, locusts, darkness, and plague on the firstborn. With each plague, Pharaoh's heart continues to harden, and he is nowhere near agreeing to let the Israelites go. God then instructs the Israelites to put blood from sheep they slaughter on their doorframes of their house:

> "On that same night, I will pass through Egypt and strike down every firstborn of both people and animals, and I will bring judgment on all the gods of Egypt, I am the Lord. The blood will be a sign for you on the houses where you are, and when I see the blood, I will pass over you. No destructive plague will touch you when I strike Egypt." . . . "During the night Pharaoh summoned Moses and Aaron and said "Up! Leave my people, you and the Israelites! Go, worship the Lord as you have requested. Take your flocks and herds, as you have said, and go. And also bless me." The Egyptians urged the people to hurry

and leave the country. "For otherwise," they said, "we will all die!" (Exod. 12:12–13, 31–33)

Finally, the Israelites are seeing light at the end of the tunnel! God has shown them he cares for them by stomping on their enemy in numerous and miraculous ways. For us in our journey today, this would be how he pieces our life together (that the world would view as just a coincidence). Those are the moments we mentioned before when you think, "This can only be from God." The worship song you hear in church that word-for-word mimics your present situation. Or the warm love God surrounds you with as He brings people who have conquered what you are faced with into your life. I recently had an eye-opening "that can only be God" moment I'd love to share:

My daughter was diagnosed with epilepsy last year, and it was a very scary experience as we did not know what was going on. Since this experience, I have been really having to work on my anxiety of her overall health. "What if they never go away?" Or, "What if the medicine stops working?" If I am not careful, I can honestly place myself in an anxiety-filled mind-set and help myself onto a hamster wheel. I knew in my heart that obviously God is in control and that I needed to work on my thoughts and go to my fortress. I decided to try out a mom's group near me and attempt to meet some nice Christian friends since I was brand-new to the area. This particular morning, I was feeling very anxious about my daughter's health, so I opened my Bible and found *wings* in the concordance. I wanted to look up *strength* or *weary*, but *wings* stood out to me so I gave it a go, and what it led me to made my jaw drop:

> Do you not know? Have you not heard? The Lord is the everlasting God, the Creator of the ends of the Earth. HE will not grow tired or weary, and his understanding no one can fathom. He gives strength to the weary and increases the power of the weak. Even youths grow tired and weary, and young men stumble and fall; but those who hope in the Lord will renew their strength.

117

They will soar on wings like Eagles; they will run and not grow weary, they will walk and not be faint.(Isa. 40:28–31)

This hit me like God was directly speaking to me personally. "Hannah, do you not remember? Haven't I told you through all of your experiences with fear and anxiety that I, the everlasting God, have this under control? Maelin is mine, I have a plan for her even though she has had some obstacles in her physical body. I will renew her strength." I was in such awe that I highlighted these verses and read them over and over again. I then went to the mom's group and a woman opened up with a testimony on how her daughter had contracted a virus and was hospitalized. She went on to say how hard it was to overcome fear and realize that God held her daughter in His hands. She then read Isaiah 40:28–31 and I froze. I could not believe the similarities in not only the story, but the Bible verses! I sobbed my face off and grabbed her after to tell her that God had used her to speak to me. The awesome thing is I had taken a picture of the verse so I could remember it if I stumbled again, so I was able to show her. She told me that it was totally God, and that my daughter would be fine. This is God fighting for you, stepping out and holding your hand and strengthening you. Utilizing other people's stories and Bible verses to correlate with you. That is God. Someday I believe in my heart you will be that person that is heard by someone in need. Someone who needs to see the outcome of what following God out of their pit looks like.

Here in Exodus God is stepping out, making himself present and holding the Israelite's hand out of Egypt:"All the Israelites did just what the Lord had commanded Moses and Aaron. And on that very day the Lord brought the Israelites out of Egypt by their divisions" (Exod. 12:50–51).

The Israelites begin their journey as God instructs them where to go, and they are ready for battle. They have gotten over the hump and have accepted that God is in fact fighting for them and that he is truly rescuing them. But then we are faced with a big obstacle as God arranges his plan and positions the Israelites in Exodus 14:2–9:

Tell the Israelites to turn back and encamp near Pi Hahiroth, between Migdol and the sea. They are to encamp by the sea, directly opposite Ball Zephon. Pharaoh will think, "The Israelites are wandering around the land in confusion, hemmed in by the desert." And I will harden Pharaoh's heart, and he will pursue them. But I will gain glory for myself through Pharaoh and all his army, and the Egyptians will know that I am the Lord. So, the Israelites did this. When the King of Egypt was told that the people had fled, Pharaoh and his officials changed their minds about them and said, "What have we done? We have let the Israelites go and have lost their services!" So he had his chariot made ready and took his army with him. He took six hundred of the best chariots of Egypt, with officers over all of them. The Lord hardened the heart of Pharaoh King of Egypt, so that he pursued the Israelites, who were marching boldly. The Egyptians—all Pharaoh's horses and chariots, horsemen and troops—pursued the Israelites and overtook them as they camped by the sea near Pi Hahiroth, opposite of Baal Zephon.

Just because the Egyptians fled their strong desire to control the Israelites, doesn't mean they were going to stick to it. Remember how we talked about Satan fleeing from Jesus and waiting for a more "opportune time?" The Israelites were able to temporarily make Satan flee, but he comes back for more as the Egyptians are changing their minds. This is why it is so important to stay armored and prepared for battle at all times. With each step in the opposite direction of Egypt, the threat grows more from Satan. They are promised by God with a destination flowing with milk and honey, and Satan is going to do everything to stop this from happening.

As Pharaoh approached, the Israelites looked up, and there were the Egyptians, marching after them. They were terrified and cried out to the Lord. "They said to Moses, "Was it because there were no graves in Egypt that you brought us to the desert to die? What have you done to us by bringing us out of Egypt? Didn't we say to you in Egypt, 'Leave us alone; let us serve the Egyptians'? It would have been better for us to serve the Egyptians than to die in the desert!" (Exod. 14:10–12)

Again, this is us as we slowly move away from our comfort zone in our depression as opposition increases. Their faith is so small that even after all that God had done for them, they still think it is better to go back to slavery and misery. They are giving up on God before trusting Him to get them through.

"Moses answered the people, "Do not be afraid. Stand firm and you will see the deliverance the Lord will bring you today. The Egyptians you see today you will never see again. The Lord will fight for you; you need only to be still." Then the Lord said to Moses,

Why are you crying out to me? Tell the Israelites to move on. Raise your staff and stretch out your hand over the sea to divide the water so that the Israelites can go through the sea on dry ground. I will harden the hearts of the Egyptians so that they will go in after them. And I will gain glory through Pharaoh and all his army, through his chariots and his horsemen. The Egyptians will know that I am the Lord when I gain glory through Pharaoh, his chariots and his horsemen . . . Then Moses stretched out his hand over the sea, and all that night the Lord drove the sea back with a strong east wind and turned it into dry land. The waters were divided, and the

Israelites went through the sea on dry ground, with a wall of water on their right and on their left.(Exod. 14:13–18, 21–22)

God is miraculously creating a way through the obstacle of water by splitting the sea and allowing the Israelites to walk on dry ground to escape the hand of the Egyptians. Can you imagine what this must have looked like? The fear these people must have experienced as they traveled into this unknown. This is so symbolic of their absolute departure from their old life of slavery, but God doesn't stop there:

The Egyptians pursued them, and all Pharaoh's horses and chariots and horsemen followed them into the sea. During the last watch of the night the Lord looked down from the pillar of fire and cloud at the Egyptian army and threw it into confusion. He jammed the wheels of their chariots so that they had difficulty driving. And the Egyptians said, "Let's get away from the Israelites! The Lord is fighting for them against Egypt." Then the Lord said to Moses, "Stretch out your hand over the sea so that the waters may flow back over the Egyptians and their chariots and horsemen." Moses stretched out his hand over the sea, and at daybreak the sea went back to its place. The Egyptians were fleeing toward it, and the Lord swept them into the sea. The water flowed back and covered the chariots and horsemen—the entire army of Pharaoh that had followed the Israelites into the sea. Not one of them survived. But the Israelites went through the sea on dry ground, with a wall of water on their right and on their left. That day the Lord saved Israel from the hands of the Egyptians, and Israel saw the Egyptians lying dead on the shore.

And when the Israelites saw the mighty hand of
the Lord displayed against the Egyptians, the
people feared the Lord and put their trust in him
and in Moses his servant.(Exod. 14:23–31)

Again, I apologize for the amount of scripture, but it is so
important. Remember, scripture is a weapon in spiritual warfare,
and I warned you we were going to battle together. This is crucial to understand the lengths that God went through to save the
Israelites. The detail he incorporated is just incredible and could have
only been thought out by Him. He went over and beyond to make
known that He was indeed keeping His covenant with them. What
is crazy to me is that it took this exact moment for the Israelites to
finally believe God was fighting for them, even after the ten plagues
and word spoken through Moses and Aaron. They are like, "Okay,
yeah, God means business now." It only took parting the Red Sea
and crushing their enemy to get them to this place of belief, but
they made it! And God kept chasing them even though their doubt
increased with each set back. I'd be a hypocrite to judge them. We all
would. I remind myself to trust God during hard times constantly, as
it easily is misplaced with fear. You would think after this life-chang-
ing experience the Israelites would maintain a high level of trust from
here on out, but this unfortunately is not the case. You would also
think after the pit God pulled me out of that I would have an unwav-
ering amount of trust and I would banish fear in the entrance of my
mind. Unfortunately, Satan does not quit, and we will face trials of
many kinds.

Now that my daughter is getting to an age of better understanding of some things, I have been telling her a little about Satan. I try
relating it to little things she struggles with, and I bring Jesus into the
conversation to show her his love. The examples I used for her were
along the lines of being disrespectful to a friend or lying to someone.
One day she came up to me with full honesty and said, "Mommy,
I am trying to not let Satan make me upset, but he keeps coming
back." Oh, her little sweet heart. She is right, he does come back, but
we know our job and more importantly we know our God! The good

news is, the more and more we grow in our faith and trust in God, the less impact these trials will have on us. I love looking back at what I conquered as a reference to remind myself that I got through such a difficult time and can do the same again.

The Israelites are in such bliss that they sing a song to the Lord in worship. The lyrics include the events that took place when God saved them from the Egyptians with thankfulness to Him. They had lived in Egypt for 430 years, and they were finally free of their physical chains. We are similar to this today, when we are on the mountain top we will sing praise of thankfulness out to God. Where we get stuck is forgetting that we go through valleys in life to get to mountain tops, and more valleys are on the horizon.

Moses led the Israelites from the Red Sea as they came to a desert. They experienced three days of not having any water to drink and were becoming desperate. They reached Marah where the water was not drinkable because of its bitter taste. The people grumbled against Moses asking him what in the world are they to drink? Moses takes this uncertainty to God. He shows Moses a piece of wood that was thrown into the water and the water became fit to drink. Sometimes in our valleys, we are just questioning God based upon our current circumstances. These people thought they had already gone through enough by escaping Egypt, but now this? I am sure Job was thinking the same thing! One of his problems would have been enough for me to be like, "Seriously, God?" I do it all of the time now, especially when it comes to our finances. We will think we are all set and stable, but then we will get hit with a forgotten tax bill and we are back to square one. But you know what, God always provides. There hasn't been one time that we ended up on the streets because of this. God stepped in and fought for us. Sometimes it would just be my grandmother giving me money because I was on her heart. That can only be God!

Water is provided in the desert for the Israelites, as a sign that God hasn't failed them yet. Once the water became purified, the Lord spoke into the situation:

> There the Lord issued a ruling and instruction for them and put them to the test. He said, "If you listen carefully to the Lord your God and do what is right in his eyes, if you pay attention to his commands and keep all his decrees, I will not bring on you any of the diseases I brought on the Egyptians, for I am the Lord who heals you." (Exod. 15:25–26)

Oh, but the Israelites are still missing that God always provides as they are continuing to complain about their situation: "In the desert, the whole community grumbled against Moses and Aaron. The Israelites said to them, 'If only we had died by the Lord's hand in Egypt! There we sat around pots of meat and ate all the food we wanted but you have brought us out into this desert to starve this entire assembly to death'" (Exod. 16:2–3).

God had just recently told these people that if they listened and did right in His eyes by keeping His commands, then he would not allow the diseases to touch them, and He will heal them. What are they so concerned about? How hard is it to just listen to God and follow Him knowing that He will take care of you? Well, it's just like how we in our depression. We read promises from God in the word, yet we still don't trust Him at times. The moment I was in when I felt God speaking to me through that woman's testimony, I was in full trust of God. Fear wasn't even a threat in my mind, my eyes were on God. But not too long after that, my daughter had to get tubes in her ears, and I was back to panicking and fearful thoughts. Satan was trying so hard to instill memory loss in me, so I fled to my fortress. I was still a tiny bit nervous as any parent would be, but I remembered she is God's child and He has it under control. It's so amazing when you can hand your responsibility of worrying over to God. Let Him take it from you. He can handle it.

The Israelites are once again admitting that they feel they would be better off dead in Egypt than in this terrible place. "There we sat around pots of meat and ate all the food *we wanted*." To me this signifies that they left something they remember being comfortable in, even though it wasn't where God wanted them. Maybe you're thinking to yourself, "Laying in my bed sleeping my depression away was much more comfortable than all of this work for crying out loud! I'd much rather take a break with this and just go back to my old self." You may have heard the phrase, "If it were easy, everyone would be doing it." Well, this is true for our trials in life, its hard stuff. Someone once told me, "I am tired of being strong." I totally sympathized for this individual because they had been through some physically, mentally, and emotionally rough conditions you wouldn't wish upon anyone. I had a hard time coming up with a response. I felt their pain radiating off them. But who they are today, and the things they conquered validate their phenomenal calling in life. Not only have they followed God through the valleys, but they are a living testimony with the ability to reach so many people under similar circumstances. And their strength in God now, you better believe it's big!

God heard the Israelites as they cry about the state they are in and how they had food in Egypt, so He once again steps in for His children: "Then the Lord said to Moses, 'I will rain down bread from heaven for you. The people are to go out each day and gather enough for that day. In this way I will test them and see whether they will follow my instructions'" (Exod. 16:4).

God is working on their hearts and minds as He is saying, "Enough for that day." They want results right now, and they want enough food to be comfortable with. Bread one day at a time is extremely different than endless pots of meat. This is what Jesus is teaching in Matthew 6:25–34 about being anxious. Now, this was written in the New Testament, way after the Israelite's story, but I just want to go over it again so you can see the similarities:

> Therefore I tell you, do not be anxious about
> your life, what you will eat or what you will drink,
> nor about your body, what you will put on. Is not
> life more than food, and they body more than
> clothing? Look at the birds of the air: they neither
> sow nor reap nor gather into barns, and yet your

heavenly Father feeds them. Are you not of more value than they? And which of you by being anxious can add a single hour to his span of life? And why are you anxious about clothing? Consider the lilies of the field, how they grow: they neither toil nor spin, yet I tell you, even Solomon in all his glory was not arrayed like one of these. But if God so clothes the grass of the field, which today is alive and tomorrow is thrown into the oven, will he not much more clothe you, O you of little faith? Therefore, do not be anxious saying, 'What shall we eat? What shall we drink? Or 'What shall we wear?' For the Gentiles seek after all these things, and your heavenly Father knows that you need them all. But seek first the kingdom of God and his righteousness, and all these things will be added to you. "Therefore do not be anxious about tomorrow, for tomorrow will be anxious for itself. Sufficient for the day is its own trouble.

I love that Jesus says not to worry about tomorrow. We have enough to handle today. Well, how are we to view tomorrow then? This is a perfect example of puzzle pieces you can fit together out of the Bible when we need answers. Philippians 3:13–14 says, "Brothers, I do not consider that I have made it my own. But one thing I do: forgetting what lies behind and straining forward to what lies ahead, I press on toward the goal for the prize of the upward call of God in Jesus Christ."

We are to forget our past troubles, live in the present moment, and have our eyes on God with regard to tomorrow. We don't know what tomorrow will bring, but the God we love does. The Israelites are stuck on reverse as they cling to their past and the comfort they thought it brought them even while they were slaves. They are definitely not living in the present as it is consumed with what-ifs about the unforeseen future. There is more detail on this daily provision of bread in Exodus 16:31–32, 35:

The people of Israel called the bread manna. It was white like coriander seed and tasted like wafers made with honey. Moses said, "This is what the Lord has commanded: 'Take an omer of manna and keep it for the generations to come, so they can see the bread I gave you to eat in the wilderness when I brought you out of Egypt.'" . . . The Israelites ate manna forty years, until they came to a land that was settled; they ate manna until they reached the border of Canaan.

They are getting tired of these conditions. This same bread they are to eat every day is getting old. Continuously complaining and regretting following Moses, and still not trusting God to fulfill His promise. They are getting nowhere by having this mind-set. It is causing them to be at a standstill mentally, spiritually, and physically. They leave the "Desert of Sin," traveling to each place the Lord called them to. They end up camping at a place called Rephidim, and again there is no water to drink in Exodus 17:2–3:

So they quarreled with Moses and said, "Give us water to drink." Moses replied, "Why do you quarrel with me? Why do you put the Lord to the test?" But the people were thirsty for water there, and they grumbled against Moses. They said, "Why did you bring us up out of Egypt to make us and our children and livestock die of thirst?"

This astounds me, especially since God had already provided clean water for them already. How could they not trust Him by now? We are seeing a repetitious pattern here, much like what we have talked about with our own negative habits of the mind. We have a fear, we freak out, cry out to God, He steps in and miraculously fights for us, and we get over a big obstacle. Then we go on a bit coasting with that peace. Then boom it hits again, and yet we have forgotten what God did for us the last time. We see here that the Israelites are not fleeing to their fortress as they are grumbling and complaining to Moses instead of trusting God. This is reflective of us going to our close friends and family before God and expecting them to do things for us only God can do. Moses ends up crying out to God explaining that he is unsure what to do with these people. He admits they are almost ready to stone him, because they are so angry and confused. God commands Moses to go out in front of the people with his staff and strike the rock at Horeb, and water will flow from it.

God gives the Ten Commandments to the Israelites, with laws to abide by and offerings explained in detail. I am sure there was some eye-rolling going on by the Israelites as this probably was viewed as more "work" for them. They had already felt like they were dying in the wilderness, now God was going to tell them how to behave? At this point, the Israelites felt entitled to freedom, and didn't think they owed anything.

God tells Moses to send some of their leaders to explore the land of Canaan, which He had planned all along to give to the Israelites:

> When Moses sent them to explore Canaan, he said, "Go up through the Negev and on into the hill country. See what the land is like and whether the people who live there are strong or weak, few or many. What kind of land do they live in? Is it good or bad? What kind of towns do they live in? Are they unwalled or fortified? How is the soil? Is it fertile or poor? Are there trees in it or not? Do your best to bring back some of the fruit of the land." (Num. 13:17–20)

I am not quite sure of the specific reasons God wanted them to explore, but I view this as a test. The Israelites have been through so much turmoil that they are becoming doubtful of the promised land being desirable, even if it's where God wants them. This is quite a long check list of things to make sure of, and I don't see a whole lot of trust involved.

I can totally relate to these anxiety-filled unknowns of where you are about to live physically. Being a military family, we didn't have much control over where our orders landed us. I remember when my husband had first told me we were to be stationed in Virginia. I was in the break room at work, seven months pregnant and full of excitement and fear. I had only driven through the state and even at that didn't pay much attention to specifics. This decision was out of my hands, and we just had to trust God that He would make a way for us there. I looked online at every little aspect of the surrounding area. I researched crime, churches, housing, schools, parks, etc. I even went the extra mile in looking up forums while obsessing over reviews on the area, especially the negative. I would read about a crime someone witnessed and I would get all sweaty and panicky and obsess over it. We had a lot of responsibility here, and I needed to find a safe area to raise our brand-new baby. Now there is a difference between being knowledgeable of an area and having anxiety attacks over the fears of the unknowns. At the end of the day, there was nothing I could do to change where we were headed, my husband signed a military contract that we committed to. At this point, I can invest some time in being aware of our new home while trusting God to protect and guide us. I eventually put a Bible verse decal on my wall for this reminder:"Have I not commanded you? Be strong and courageous. Do not be afraid; do not be discouraged, for the Lord your God will be with you wherever you go?" (Josh. 1:9).

If Canaan was where God was promising them, what was the purpose of reporting its negative conditions? God is crystal clear of the exact place He has been leading them to, and they are still leery. Let's check out their report on the land:

> They came back to Moses and Aaron and the whole Israelites community at Kadesh in the desert of Paran. There they reported to them and to the whole assembly and showed them the fruit of the land. They gave Moses this account: "We went into the land to which you sent us, and it does flow with milk and honey! Here is its fruit.

> But the people who live there are powerful, and the cities are fortified and very large . . . Then Caleb silenced the people before Moses and said, "We should go up and take possession of the land, for we can certainly do it." But the men who had gone up with him said, "We can't attack those people; they are stronger than we are. And they spread among the Israelites a bad report about the land they had explored. They said, "The land we explored devours those living in it. All the people we saw there are great size . . . We seemed like grasshoppers in our own eyes, and we looked the same to them." (Num. 13:26–28, 30–33)

The Israelites are really maintaining their doubt as they saw what God had promised with their own eyes, but that sight was overshadowed by the giants. Had they not learned that God is bigger than any giant that they encounter? They have already physically seen the beauty in the land, but their fear is forming tunnel vision. I try to envision placing myself in their shoes on the trek back to unveil their findings. They were probably obsessing over it, and how they were going to convince everyone else that it was not a good idea. We have giants too in our lives, and they seem to have the ability to crush us if we let them. Fear is a giant, anxiety is a giant, depression is a giant, sin is a giant, etc. But we have scripture and the promises of God that He has a perfect plan for us centered on trust, especially the promise of heaven. If we listen to the Holy Spirit, we will have guidance throughout our journey. Some paths are narrow and less traveled. They aren't popular as they seem less enticing to the world: "Enter through the narrow gate. For wide is the gate and broad is the road that leads to destruction, and many enter through it" (Matt. 7:13).

I am not going to lie, if I saw giants in the land God was calling me to reside, I would flee. Our flesh desires catering to itself and its comforts. The Israelites are tired of their living conditions. The last thing they want to do is take on giants. A man named Caleb believes they can take possession of the land and declares, "For we can certainly do it." I am sure he is taking into account all that God had done for them already. He had provided for them thus far. If they are wishing they had died in Egypt, what do they have to lose to try? We run into another road block they create for themselves in Numbers 14:

> That night all the members of the community raised their voices and wept aloud. All the Israelites grumbled against Moses and Aaron, and the whole assembly said to them, "If only we had died in Egypt! Or in the wilderness! Why is the Lord bringing us to this land only to let us fall by the sword? Our wives and children will be taken as plunder. Wouldn't it be better for us to go back to Egypt? And they said to each other, "We should choose a leader and go back to Egypt." Then Moses and Aaron fell face down in front of the whole Israelite assembly gathered there. Joshua son of Nun, and Caleb son of Jephunneh, who were among those who had explored the land, tore their clothes and said to the entire Israelite assembly, "The land we passed through and explored is exceedingly good. If the Lord is pleased with us, he will lead us into that land, a land flowing with milk and honey, and will give it to us. Only do not rebel against the Lord. And do not be afraid of the people of the land, because we will devour them. Their protection is gone, but the Lord is with us. Do not be afraid of them." (Num. 14:1–9)

Here they go again, prolonging their stay in the wilderness as they go back to their typical response, "If only we died in Egypt!" This time though they throw out the threat of finding a qualified leader to take them back to Egypt. Satan works his way through the cracks and just tricks us to the best of his ability. These people are deceived into thinking they had an easier life being slaves! What they are missing is that God has provided the entire time and has never left them. I don't know about you but I'd rather be in the wilderness with God than bound by chains without him, even if I were in better living conditions with all of the food I needed.

Joshua and Caleb get their attention by tearing their clothes and reassuring them that the land was exceedingly good and that God would lead them into it if He was pleased with them. They are told not to be afraid of the giants because God is with them. The giants will be devoured as their protection will be absent. Moses ends up giving a play-by-play to the Israelites in hopes of opening their eyes to what God has been telling him:

> "Do not be terrified; do not be afraid of them. The Lord your God, who is going before you, will fight for you, as he did for you in Egypt, before your very eyes, and in the wilderness. There you saw how the Lord your God carried you, as a father carries his song, all the way you went until you reached this place" (Deut. 1:29–31).

> "The lord your God has blessed you in all the work of your hands. He has watched over your journey through this vast wilderness. These forty years the Lord your God has been with you, and you have lacked nothing" (Deut. 2:7).

> "Only be careful, and watch yourselves closely so that you do not forget the things your eyes have seen or let them fade from your heart as long as you live. Teach them to your children and to their children after them" (Deut. 4:9).

The Israelites are getting a lot of reminders that God will take care of them, especially after all that He has done up until this point. Also, they were told, "Watch yourselves closely so that you do not forget the things your eyes have seen." Remember Satan's love for memory loss? This is a perfect example as Moses warns them not to forget these huge miraculous things done for them!

Sadly Moses passes away; however, Joshua takes his place and God speaks to him here in Joshua 1:

> Moses my servant is dead. Now then, you and all these people, get ready to cross the Jordan River into the land I am about to give to them- to the Israelites. I will give you every place where you set your foot, as I promised Moses. Your territory will extend from the desert to Lebanon, and from the great river, the Euphrates—all the Hittite country—to the Mediterranean Sea in the west. No one will be able to stand against you all the days of your life. As I was with Moses, so I will be with you; I will never leave you nor forsake you. Be strong and courageous, because you will lead these people to inherit the land I swore to their ancestors to give them. Be strong and very courageous.(Josh. 1:2–6)

Joshua then sends two spies to look over the land, and they are told that they are feared by the people:

> I know that the Lord has given you this land and that a great fear of you has fallen on us, so that all who live in this country are melting in fear because of you. We have heard how the Lord dried up the water of the Red Sea for you when you came out of Egypt, and what you did to Sihon and Og, the two kings of the Amorites east of the Jordan, whom you completely destroyed. When we heard of it, our hearts melted in fear and everyone's courage failed because of you, for

the Lord your God in heaven above and on the
earth below.(Josh. 2:9–11)

The two spies report back to Joshua their findings: "The Lord
has surely given the whole land into our hands; all the people are
melting in fear because of us" (Josh. 2:24).

They have confirmation by word that these people are dwelling
in fear of the Israelite's presence. Wouldn't you love your "giants" to
tell you, "I am afraid of you because of what God has done for you?"
If we look back in Deuteronomy 1:2, we see the actual geological
distance their journey should have been:"It takes eleven days to go
from Horeb to Kadesh Barnea by the Mount Seri road."

They surely prolonged their time in the wilderness, all the
way to forty years. Big difference in time here! Can you imagine
if they had trusted and obeyed God from the very beginning! Not
only would their trial had been cut short, but they would have been
blessed beyond belief along the way. Whew! Thanks for sticking
around during that long visual. Go reward yourself with a refresh-
ment or nap. You deserve it for hanging in there with me!

What is so amazing about Moses, Job, and Paul is that the Bible
visually shows how drastically challenging their life was compared
to ours. If they can do it, we certainly can too! God said repetitively
that he followed through with his covenant with Abraham, Isaac, and
Jacob to remind them that He would also keep His covenant with
them. So they had physical miracles, provision, and direct word that
God had followed through many times before. Just like we have this
confirmation in the Bible and in our walk with God.

TRIALS

Trials teach us what we are; they dig up the soil, and let us see what we are made of.

—Charles Spurgeon

We have just gone over an example that displayed many trials, but what if we reach our breakthrough, but then encounter another big trial? The things I myself have been through, and my husband and I together as a couple, were numerous and undesired. I have already shared my testimony of my depression in my young adult life, but there has been so much more added to my story:

The military lifestyle was very hard for us at first, and we felt stuck. My husband signed months before we got married followed by the discovery of my pregnancy, and it was a lot at once! He had committed to six years, and I remember thinking in the second year, "I don't think I can do four more years of this!" I began to panic and I just wanted him to get out, but unfortunately that is hard to obtain without a penalty that will haunt you the rest of your career. My husband went on a deployment and missed a whole year of our daughter's life, and it was very emotional. I began to despise Virginia, and I developed my lovely tunnel vision again. This was way too hard, and it wasn't how I envisioned my future to be. I didn't have anyone bringing us meals or helping with the baby so I could have a break. Our extended family was missing out on her life, and it was so hard for me to accept. Again, I went back to the mind-set of needing my mom and dad to function or I wasn't going to make it. This then was hurtful toward my husband as he strived to be all that

I needed, and it clearly didn't seem like enough at the time. I complained about everything, the cost of living, the traffic, the heat in the summer, the taxes, the rude people, the bugs, etc. I was surely in another wilderness full of bitterness, and I was allowing the giants to scare me off, even though God was providing some amazing things to bless us with.

I became weary as a parent while my husband was constantly gone, and I really let it get to me. I started to think I wasn't cut out for this job, and I didn't deserve my child. This caught me by surprise, as I had been a nanny for years and was pretty good at it. Kids would beg their parents to go out so I could come play with them. I really thought I would have it all together, but the situation I was in made me think otherwise. Satan tries his best to burrow into young parents' minds especially. We are responsible for human life. It's a big deal! For myself, my anxiety would try to build walls for me to run into which stopped me from reaching joy. I avoided so many things in order to avoid my anxiety alerting me in an emergency-like fashion. I started thinking to myself, "Do I even love my child enough?" I finally got to my fortress as I recognized how silly this all was. Looking back, I found this bulleted in my journal for when I needed reminders:

- "Get up, this is just anxiety. It's happened before and you got over it!"
- Read your note cards.
- Get up early, spend time with God.
- Look at "my little love" picture if you have doubts of being a good mom. (This is a picture of my daughter as a newborn baby asleep on my chest.)
- Watch the home video, look at the way you look at your daughter.
- It is okay to get frustrated when she acts up. Don't be afraid of anger. Learn how to go to God.
- She is so close to saying, "Mama."
- Don't have limitations.
- You are confident.

Once again, my lovely fear of going crazy was lingering, and what was so frustrating is that I knew I had already gotten over this thought before. I wrote this list while in my fortress, when my mind was clear and confident in my breakthrough. I knew I would be faced with my anxiety again, and I needed to be prepared. During this time, my husband was on deployment, so my mind was firing on all cylinders trying to distract me from the emotions that caused. I was missing my husband and concerned for his safety. I got through that season with God as we approached my husband's homecoming, and it was blissful. I finally felt back to myself as we got back into a family rhythm. We ended up becoming pregnant after he returned, and we were more than excited to add to the family! Maelin was at the perfect age to have a sibling join her, and we just could not wait. We found out we were going to have a baby boy, and we began planning for his little life. I started buying boy clothes and hanging them up in his newly made pirate themed nursery. We went back and forth with names and how it would sound next to Maelin's. My husband had dreams of taking him in truck rides, fishing, and being manly in the woods.

I started having some problems with my pregnancy and ended up on bed rest for ten weeks. Obviously, my anxiety shot through the roof. My pregnancy was flawless with my daughter, and this was foreign to me. It became extremely difficult with a two-and-a-half-year-old, especially our bouncy little active explorer. My mom and dad actually came down to get her and brought her up to Michigan to give me a little break. One night I told my husband something didn't feel right, and I ended up in the ER. I waited in triage and was finally told I was dilated at only twenty-two weeks. I crumbled into this spinning vortex of fear. How could this be? I was admitted and was in a bed for two weeks, getting steroid shots, holding still, and praying for contractions to hold off. I wasn't even allowed to shower, so my husband had to give me a sponge bath in my hospital bed.

We had no family in the area, and I begged Chris to sleep in my room every night. There was one night in particular he had to go home, and the second he left the room I just started to panic. Five minutes later, I find myself rolling my eyes at the sound of a knock on the door, but in walks this woman not sporting scrubs, but a Bible. She introduced herself as Beverly the Chaplin and was a little reserved at first as she felt for a response in my acceptance. Up until this point my life, the last two weeks were extremely medical. Hospital noises, questions, gloves, blood drawings, statistics, concerned faces, hospital food, etc. But God showed up through Beverly and fought for me! She was "my people," and suddenly it didn't matter that she was a stranger. God was speaking through her. We talked for more than she had planned, as she still had more patients to visit down the hall. But we laughed, cried, and prayed, and I knew from that moment on that God was with me. He didn't stop there. We became family with every single nurse that was assigned to me. There were nurses who had families to go home to after they clocked out, but they chose to come and sit with us in our room. We laughed, joked, and exchanged numbers and hugs. They told me success stories of previous women that were able to make it far enough in their pregnancy for the baby to survive. In a room that Satan once tried to occupy, God took over. My friend that I had just recently met in a maternity store was the only friend that visited me in the hospital. Think about that, I wouldn't have even met her if I wasn't pregnant. That can only be God.

I remember feeling a gush and being sent to the high-risk doctor for an ultrasound. The tech was very quiet and expressed concerned through her expressions. The doctor came in the room with the results, "You have ruptured and the baby does not have much fluid left. You will need antibiotics to prevent infection, and we will just have to hope he hangs on long enough to grow." For some reason, I had this peace that I cannot describe in words. Don't get me wrong, I was still scared, but it was not controlling me. It was like I was just flowing with the news, riding the waves, but they weren't crashing into me. I got wheeled back to the room and had all the nurses come hug and encourage us.

I started contracting at twenty-three weeks and five days and ended going into labor. He was breech, so I decided to try and save him by doing an emergency C-section. Doctors thought I was crazy to put myself through a very invasive surgery for such a tiny baby, but we had to try. One of the nurses left her station and consoled Chris in the hallway as they prepped me in the OR. This woman went out of her way to stand right next to us and explain what to expect during the delivery. She even took pictures of his birth for us! We were told he would come out gray and might not make any sound, but he came out pink screaming his little head off. The NICU staff took amazing care of him and whisked him off to the NICU. He weighed one pound and seven ounces, and his name was Sawyer James Parkison. He had blond hair with a little swirl on the top and bright blue eyes.

There were many ups and downs, and miracles we were blessed with. He proved the doctors wrong on many occasions. He was so brave. All the nurses and doctors in the NICU became very close to us, and they loved our boy to the point of fighting over who got to take care of him each day. On the night of Chris's birthday, we visited him and he had such a good day! Chris decided to say a prayer in the parking garage, and oh, did I not want to hear it at the time. He said, "God, thank you so much for Sawyer. Each day has been a blessing. If he is going to make it, please give us a sign, but if he isn't please take him to be with you." See, the entire time we had been praying for him to be healed here, who wouldn't? But Chris's prayer was bowing down to God's will and surrendering to His plan even if it hurt our hearts. Although I wasn't comfortable with that prayer at the time, my husband took a big leap in his faith as he became a godly leader for our family that night. We got a call at 4:30 a.m. from the hospital saying his heart was failing, and he didn't have much time left. We rushed to the hospital and loved on him as much as we could. Sawyer went into cardiac arrest and went to be with Jesus on October 10, 2013. It was the hardest day I have ever experienced in my life. I remember Chris finally speaking up through his tears, "God answered my prayer. Sawyer is fully healed in heaven."

He lived for thirty days, but in those thirty days, he touched the lives of more people than I ever could have fathomed. People all over the world were praying, some telling me it was their first encounter with God. While this wasn't the outcome we all hoped for, Chris and I remained steadfast in our faith and trust in God. We had such a peace, even though to the world we had every right to turn from God after experiencing such loss. We were able to truthfully display our faith in the situation, and there was not an ounce of fake in it. Yes, I was sad and confused, but I knew the God who provided comfort in my pain and answers to my questions. There is no doubt in my mind that there is a little bouncy, feisty bright blond-headed boy up there on the lap of Jesus, and someday I will get to hold him again. I know these are stories that depressed people are very sensitive to and don't feel uplifted at all. I totally get it, but I can't tell you about the mountain I climbed if I leave out the valley I conquered.

I remember calling my therapist and thanking her for helping me get to a place where I can handle situations as drastic as this without slipping back into a depression. I am grateful that I had previously been through something that taught me about running to God, or else I am not sure I would have made it after such loss. We don't go through these trials without God having a reason for them on the other side. After we lost him, the entire NICU just surrounded us with love in phone calls, hugs, visits, and gifts. We went into that hospital without family nearby and left with an entire new family of hospital staff members. That can only be God.

Don't worry, things are about to get good. I can't end on a very sad note in a book on attacking depression and anxiety! My husband was nearing the end of his contract and we decided to try for another baby. Of course, my anxiety was trying to get the best of me, "What if that happens again!" I found out I was pregnant on the year anniversary of Sawyer's heavenly birthdate. Oh, the fear and excitement mixed in my mind and heart. I had some big giants during this time, but I leaned into and trusted God that no matter what happened, it was His plan. My pregnancy was flawless, and I was monitored by the doctors as I was considered high risk. We as a family all went in to my appointment one day as the doctor had confirmed that I was far enough along to find out the sex. My husband as a man had such high hopes for having a son and still yearned for one. Expectations with a son were lost with the loss of Sawyer. We were on pins and needles as the doctor said, "Well, the legs are crossed but I am more than certain this is a girl." We all left the room grateful, but we had a little bit of disappointment present, at least we had a ton of girl stuff! My twenty-week scan approached and we all went again to see the baby on the ultrasound. We all didn't expect anything but a girl, but we were then told, "It's a boy!" I cannot even explain how I felt in words, so I am not going to even try. God provided fully! He didn't even have to take it to that level, but He did! We were entirely shocked and just over the moon with the news. We told everyone, and tears were not missing on anyone's face. We had a 9-lb 15-oz baby boy on a beautiful June day that we named Auden Sawyer. Oh, was he gorgeous and perfect! I remember just looking at him in the hospital bin. I couldn't believe he was thriving and healthy. It felt like a dream. The thankfulness I still feel in my heart today will never go away. Every time I look at him I am reminded of God's provision and love. He and Maelin are miracles.

God still had some work to do in me, as I still was not content in Virginia. Even after all of this provision, I still desired to go home. I remember our pastor one day saying, "You are meant to be in Hampton Roads, Virginia, for a reason." It made me so mad. I thought, "No, we are not. What do you know?" You see, because we were away from family, I felt like we were wasting our time down there. I was prolonging my stay in the wilderness as I was easily forgetting all God had done so far. Through all of this, we were building our own family roots in Virginia without me even realizing it. We were heavily strengthened through living a military lifestyle and gained a sense of closeness as a little family. We valued our time together more than a family who sees each other on a daily basis. I branched out and forced myself to make friends when I would have just clung to family at home. We developed our own independent routine, when I would have relied on my parents to do things for us. We gained amazing neighbors that loved on our kids and were there for us with a pie at our front door on holidays we were alone. Home was my Egypt, and I thought it was our answer. "This cannot be God's plan for us. It has been one thing right after another! We are better off at home where it's comfortable and familiar with family."

Chris's contract had come to an end, and we moved back home and we were comfortable, for a little bit. Obviously, we were loving the family time we had missed and the familiarity that we longed for while in Virginia. But as time slipped further and further away, our desire to be in Virginia, our family's "home," increased. I felt the closest to God I have ever felt in my while life living there, and it warms my heart just thinking about it. God placed His perfect plan upon our lives, and I kicked and screamed just like the Israelites in the wilderness. I didn't trust His plan at first, but I am so grateful for it. Now when Chris and I experience new trials, we know the strength in God because of the obstacles we have conquered!

WHAT TO DO WHEN
TRIALS KEEP COMING

So, you see, I honestly thought after my first episode with depression that I was all set and had done my time. I figured God would just let me coast through the remainder of my life with little to no hardship, but that's just not how things work. Let's check out what the Bible says about trials here:

> Consider it pure joy, my brothers and sisters, whenever you face trials of many kinds, because you know that the testing of your faith produces perseverance. Let perseverance finish its work so that you may be mature and complete, not lacking anything. If any of you lacks wisdom, you should ask God, who gives generously to all without finding fault, and it will be given to you. But when you ask, you must believe and not doubt, because the one who doubts is like a wave of the sea, blown and tossed by the wind. That person should not expect to receive anything from the Lord. Such a person is double-minded and unstable in all they do.(James 1:2–8)

So we are to immerse ourselves in pure joy when we are confronted with a trial? This sounds completely backward, right? To the world, it is most certainly backward. You would be considered crazy if you were to be happy about going through something hard. But, as we mature in our faith and trust in God, we learn what this really means. If trials are presented to us, God considers us strong enough to make it through them. With each trial, He is preparing you for a new level in your faith.

We have already discussed how He will never give us more than we can handle with Him by our side, so what is there to be so distraught about? When Sawyer was still with us, I learned to see the small miracles that presented themselves within the storm. Each day was a blessing, and we started thanking God just for each day in itself. I started realizing that some parents lose their babies before even meeting them or struggle with infertility. Here I was, able to be with my son and get to know him for thirty days. He loved to be read to, his numbers improved when we read books to him as the nurses watched in wonder. We got to display our faith to so many, and I began to feel honored that God chose us to be his parents.

These verses in James also point out that if you lack wisdom, you should ask God, but you must believe and not doubt. This is considered being double-minded and unstable in God's eyes. It is okay to be confused during times of trial, and if you desire wisdom, you can ask God for it. The awesome thing is God is not confused:"-For God [who is the source of their prophesying] is not a God of confusion and disorder but of peace and order" (1 Cor. 14:33).

As long as you are not double-minded and unstable by unbelief and doubt, then you will be blessed in His time. This was totally the Israelite's problem. They were surely double-minded. They asked and pleaded to be removed from their situation but were filled with consistent and stubborn doubt. When we had our son Auden, we were in a tiny wilderness. About a week into his life, he developed jaundice pretty badly. My husband was really taking this hard, as we had just been through the loss of Sawyer. I remember him actually saying, "I knew it was too good to be true," referring to our perfect delivery and Auden's clean bill of health. Now, I am not blaming Chris's feelings, but this has doubt written all over it. At the time, it made me angry, because I wanted to be hopeful and I felt my anxiety pulling me down to a level of vulnerability. By him saying this, it was admitting that we were doubting before believing God would keep him healthy and thriving. We finally got to our fortress and got into survival mode and had strength to get him through that rough patch with God.

Once we began entering into our trust, God just made it go so smoothly. We were blessed with an amazing pediatrician that was available after hours directly to her cell phone! One Sunday afternoon, we got the test results back from the blood work, and the levels were the highest they had been. Typically, doctors are not available on the weekend, but this woman was doing Google searches from her home to find us a service that would bring a bilirubin blanket to our home. She also calmed my husband and I down and told us Auden was going to be fine. She happened to be a Christian as well and incorporated God in comforting us. That can only be God. Because my husband and I have been through so much and held firm to our strength and trust in God, people are amazed. Our life is a living testimony of God's love and provision. I am sure we will encounter more trials throughout our marriage and parenthood, but we are set on a firm foundation!

CONTENTMENT

I rejoice greatly in the Lord that at last you have renewed your concern for me. Indeed, you have been concerned, but you had no opportunity to show it. I am not saying this because I am in need, for I have learned to be content whatever the circumstance. I know what it is to be in need, and I know what it is to have plenty. I have learned the secret of being content in any and every situation, whether well fed or hungry, whether living in plenty or in want. I can do everything through him who gives me strength.

—Philippians 4:10–13

We have only talked a little about Paul, but enough to know he went through some incredibly hard times. He shares the secret in finding contentment in any circumstance. Whether poor or rich, hungry or well fed, you have no excuse to not have contentment. These temporary conditions don't alter his contentment knowing that he can do everything through Christ who gives him strength. Being content is sometimes very difficult for me, especially as an anxious person. I find myself constantly at the battle lines of presently being uncomfortable with something while waiting for change. "When this happens, everything will be better, and I will be able to relax." I have found myself actually crossing dates off my calendar with such determination to get somewhere in the future fast, while I care very little about the present moment. How terrible is that? I am wishing away time God has blessed me with, and if I think like Paul does, contentment is burrowed in the moment and I must seek it.

You can go into any assisted living home and ask an elderly person what they long for. It isn't money or material things, it is time. See, you possess something they no longer hold grasp on, your youth. Everyone goes through trials in life, but they would do anything to go back to any season in their past if it meant they could turn back time. I once saw a therapy used on elderly women with dementia, and it amazed me. They give them a baby doll to take care of. To the woman, this baby is her child and goes through all the maternal motions of being that baby's caretaker. I am literally crying as I type this. It makes me so emotional. Huge smack in the face to those who would give anything for the place I am now, as I am wishing my time away in hopes of an easier season. Commit to the present moment. It is gone so quickly.

Obviously, we are not content during depression. We are in a very fragile state. I, however, struggle with contentment whether I am depressed or not. This is where Satan strives the most for us to have memory loss and forget everything God has blessed us with. After all I have been through and gotten out of because of God. I should be content solely in the fact that I made it. Breakthrough is easily masked with the next trial we face. For years I crossed off days that brought us closer to our goal, to be free civilians. I was not content in Virginia, and I was only focusing on something I was chasing. Again, this is a slippery slope as we are missing out on the blessings in the present moment. I viewed life as just things in the way that were hurdles until we got out and moved home. I prayed for contentment many, many times, but I didn't realize that I should have been praying to activate my joy in order to blossom my contentment. I would be so jealous of other military wives who seemed invincible to what the navy brought on their family. I would ask myself, "How do they do it? How do they even like it here?" Their husbands would be out to sea, and they were just pushing through with such a calm patience that I longed for. I placed the blame on external influences rather than internal—it was the navy's and Virginia's fault. I was blind to the fact that I needed to change, not the circumstances. This is such a big misconception. We think that once the elements surrounding us change we will finally be content, for good. What's funny is I found this to be false when we moved home to Michigan, I still struggle with contentment where I fled. I spent five years away from a Michigan winter, and let me tell you, it's very rough. It is gray for months and sometimes seems inhabitable. It's so cold outside that it actually hurts your body, and you start desiring to never leave your warm, cozy home. My family had to spend a fortune on winter wear because it was unnecessary where we came from. I find it very hard to be content during this, especially with kids. I seriously go to the grocery store and want to shake people while saying, "What are we even doing here? This is miserable!" Now it has become very apparent what I should have appreciated in the place I ran from. The ironic thing is that this is what I was crossing off my present days for, what I thought would bring me happiness. Nothing was more important than hurrying life up in order to reach this, and my tunnel vision forgot a very large amount of detail in where I longed to be.

My point is, it doesn't matter where we are in life. We are capable of being content. I don't know if you have noticed, but some of the poorest people in unimaginable conditions are the happiest. My aunt and uncle have five boys and went through a season of financial hardship. I have already told you my background and that I was very blessed with an amazing childhood, so this was foreign to me. These kids would create fun activities out of nothing. It was incredible. They were always so content with the little they had. I was envious of it. Still to this day, they are so appreciative and just happy to be alive. All of them give huge bear hugs and express their love greatly in God and people.

Your contentment affects everyone you are around, and it can be contagious whether you're joyful or pitiful. I am such a people-pleaser that when someone is not content it makes me anxious, like I need to fix something for them. My poor husband listened to me complain daily down in Virginia. He has the gift of listening, but I am sure it was starting to get old. Think about how this could have been negatively affecting him. We were in our circumstances simply because of his decision to be in the military, and he began confessing that he felt guilty for getting us into the situation. I noticed that he started caring less about his job as his effort decreased. Think of how differently things could have been if I was honest about how I felt, but didn't let it ruin my contentment? He would have been less stressed, guilt free, and enjoyed it while it lasted. Don't you just wish you could turn back time? I will say it allowed me to gain wisdom in this area that obviously needed a lot of tweaking.

I have a friend who happens to be a therapist. Now, I have not talked with her about God, but from what I gather, she is not outspoken about what she believes. I cannot judge her heart, only God can, but from the outside, it isn't obvious she is a Christian. She confessed to me that she also struggles with anxiety and depression, and that she went through postpartum depression after having her baby. I was shocked, as I never would have guessed this to be an issue for someone in her profession. Doesn't she have all the answers and tools as a therapist? She told me she was constantly asked why she couldn't help herself with her education and it was making her frustrated. This is a perfect example of a huge missing piece in our healing. We can have all the medical studies, chemical imbalance fixes, and cognitive therapies, but without God, full contentment is unreachable. I wish I could just place God into the equation for my friend, but I can only be an example of Jesus Christ and share my testimony.

FRUIT OF THE SPIRIT

I was struggling recently with contentment and was trying my hardest to pinpoint the source. This anxiety wasn't like what I experienced with depression. I wasn't fully consumed in despair, but I was getting angry very easily, which could lead me down an undesirable road if not taken care of. I had been very low on patience with my children and had been allowing anger to form and consume my emotions. I remember thinking, "Why am I so angry?" I realized I needed to study and pray for my patience to be recharged and maintained. Patience is a fruit of the spirit, so I turned to the concordance and started digging.

> "But the Holy Spirit produces this kind of fruit in our lives: love, joy, peace, patience, kindness, goodness, faithfulness, gentleness, and self-control. There is no law against these things" (Gal. 5:22–23).

I am just going to call the fruit of the spirit our "power pack." There are plenty of superhero shows/movies out there for kids and adults alike. These superheroes may fly, shoot webs from their wrists, have immense strength, etc. Together they are a team of people that contribute certain attributes to obtain their goal of saving the world. If one were absent, this goal would be missed. While you are watching these heroes fight in action, you have a mental checklist that keeps track of every hero's job in pulling their weight in order to succeed. We are to have a checklist in our daily lives as well. This list contains love, joy, peace, patience, kindness, goodness, faithfulness, gentleness, and self-control.

Some of these (maybe all) are definitely not present when we struggle with anxiety and depression. When you are feeling so badly, you don't have much love for yourself. How can you love on others? Joy is certainly absent as we are depressed and are not enjoying life. Peace is totally gone as we are filled with fear and anxiety. Since we are so concentrated on ourselves, it is difficult to even care enough to be kind toward others. Goodness, what is good about our situation? If we are continuing to doubt God in getting us through, then our faith isn't present. We are not extremely gentle when we are depressed as we may lash out at people in anger. Finally, self-control? We are very weak in this area as we are allowing Satan to control our feelings. Getting out of depression centers around self-control as we are breaking these chains of slavery to Satan's lies.

You may be thinking, "How do I receive these? I ask God to give them to me all of the time?" You gained access the second you accepted Jesus as your Lord and Savior, as they are through the Spirit whom was given to us. By activating them, we are making attacks during spiritual warfare. Like the word of God and prayer, these are all very powerful weapons. When you are depressed, the majority of these have a very low battery but are charged when you reach your breakthrough. When you climb out of your pit, you will be in a "honeymoon" stage, where you feel invincible. Since we have grown in faith and trust in God through our latest trial, we aren't hit as hard and still have power in most of our attributes. This is all a part of staying armored and maintaining our mind to prevent falling into depression again. When a new trial presents itself, flee to your fortress, and then take a look around at which attribute(s) needs maintenance.

What is so awesome about the fruit of the spirit is that God doesn't just leave you guessing as to what needs to be managed, He is very direct and simple. This makes it easy for us to focus instead of wasting time searching for answers. It reminds me a lot of multiple choice tests. You can use processes of elimination for the right answer. I extremely fill-in-the-blank tests, definitely reaching in the dark with that style. Let's elaborate on each attribute to help give you a guide to follow:

Love

We hear the word *love* often, but do we know the true depth of its meaning?

> "You must love the Lord your God with all your heart, all your soul, and all your mind. This is the first and greatest commandment" (Matt. 22:37–38).

> "Love is patient and kind. Love is not jealous or boastful or proud or rude. It does not demand its own way. It is not irritable, and it keeps no record of being wronged. It does not rejoice about injustice but rejoices whenever the truth wins out. Love never gives up, never loses faith, is always hopeful, and endures through every circumstance" (1 Cor.13:4–7).

These are just two examples of scripture covering love, but the Bible is full of this word and act. It's hard to love on others when we are weary and not even liking ourselves at the moment. I am not talking about loving yourself to the point of being conceited and boastful but loving yourself to a healthy level. Again, we can get self-centered during our valleys and focus solely on the storm. This creates a growing disgust and shame of ourselves, all while slamming the door on love. Sometimes it takes showing love to someone else to break free our love for ourselves.

Joy

Let's face it, joy is well hidden while we are anxious or depressed. It is never absent on its own. It's our responsibility to find it even in the pit. We exchange our potentially joyful present moment for fear, anxiety, scary obsessive thoughts, and depression. Again, we are allowing ourselves to be slaves to something willingly.

> "Always be full of joy in the Lord. I say it again rejoice!" (Phil. 4:4).

> "The young women will dance for joy, and the men-old and young- will join in the celebration. I will turn their mourning into joy. I will comfort them and exchange their sorrow for rejoicing" (Jer. 31:13).

We have no excuse to not have joy with the promise of eternal life in heaven when we accept Jesus as our Lord and Savior. We get memory loss of this gracious gift and focus on the hardships here on earth. Think about it, we are here on this earth for a short while with some out-of-control hardships, but we aren't going to hell! There is literally light at the end of the tunnel!

Peace

> The name of the Lord is a strong tower; the
> righteous run to it and they are safe.

> —Proverbs 18:10

Peace is accessed when we reach our fortress as we feel "safe" and able of rest. Those moments when you find your way there, and you can just rest in the presence of God. If you are struggling badly with peace, you are not staying in your fortress long enough. Just like our friend Susie a while back, she thought she was all set with minimal effort, but she was just touching the outside wall. She was getting a glimpse of her fortified place, and what it held, but she didn't go inside. That's like buying a house that you have just seen the exterior of, but not knowing the interior. Just picture it with me. You have the specifics on paper in front of you, the number of bedrooms, bathrooms, updates, etc. You know its design and what it's all about, but are you at peace with your decision? You haven't even gone inside to dwell and actually get to know the place in order to feel comfortable with moving on with your decision. We have the specifics of who God is when we read the Bible or go to church, but are you meeting one on one in your fortress to the point of actually reaching peace in God?

> "Then you will experience God's peace, which exceeds anything we can understand. His peace will guard your hearts and minds as you live in Christ Jesus" (Phil. 4:7).

> "You will keep in perfect peace all who trust in you, all whose thoughts are fixed on you" (Isa. 26:3).

We spoke earlier about being double-minded. You cannot have it both ways. We can't continue to obsess over fear and anxiety while getting frustrated as to why God is not giving us peace. You have it in you already through the Holy Spirit, go to God and find rest.

Patience

As we have thoroughly discussed, the Israelite's had little to no patience in the wilderness. They were already given the word that they would make it eventually to the promised land, but it wasn't in their time. As a society today, we are centered on things happening immediately with little effort. It's in our flesh's nature. As a parent, I think patience can be lost quickly every single day if you aren't careful. We are always running late, and I want the kids to listen the first time while rushing out the door. Usually my daughter ends up finding something very random and constructive to do as we are trying to walk out the door. I have to try really hard to be patient and understanding of why she is doing this. She is a little kid full of curiosity, and she doesn't have a care in the world when it comes to time management. I bring my frustration down a lot of notches and approach her calmly. God always provides amazing moments when I am patient, things I would have missed if I were to have rushed her.

Being patient during difficult trials is very wearing. In the first five years of our marriage, we just felt like we were treading water. One thing after another, and everyone would say, "Goodness, you guys have been through more than some have in their entire life!" It's hard to be patient smack dab in the middle of the wilderness, especially when you hand the reins over to God and let go of control. This is something we are to put into His hands, and sometimes it's a test He is allowing us to go through. Maybe all He is looking for is your reaction, and then your action. There have been plenty of times the light bulb would go off in my head suddenly. I would follow God's guidance in a certain area, and I would find myself out of the weeds of a wilderness once I understood the lesson I was to learn. When we are patient, we allow God's will to take over, and it displays our trust in Him to follow through.

> "But if we look forward to something we don't have yet, we must wait patiently and confidently" (Rom. 8:25).

Kindness

It's hard to be kind toward anyone when you are feeling so lousy. You are giving all of your energy to your anxiety. When I was trying to figure out how to feel better, I felt that God put on my heart to find someone to share God with, even though I wasn't fully out of my wilderness yet. I ended up finding someone to be in a very similar situation as myself. This person was allowing their feelings to take the reins of their life, and it was crippling them. They weren't really involved with God, and I was anxious to be rejected in my offer to help. I got a copy of the book that was helping me at the time and got a good worship CD for them to listen to. I also had jotted down what I was going to say, how I was healing, and how God was pulling me through. I didn't do this because I was feeling good. I had to force my flesh to do it while I felt terrible. But I realized as I sat there with them, pouring my heart out through tears that God was utilizing me during my pain to speak to them. It made it ever clearer that what we follow is true, even in pain and suffering we can find the good. Reaching out to someone is a win-win situation. You win because you take your mind off yourself for a moment while you are helping someone else. It may take a minute to realize, but you are entering spiritual warfare and winning the battle against Satan by doing this. You are ignoring how you feel and helping someone else with the outcome of you both reaching God. The person on the receiving end also wins as they are being sought out, cared for, loved on, and given a Christ-like example before their very eyes. If you want people to want what you have in Jesus, you have to show it. Allow them, "That can be only God moments" through you. This particular person ended up calling me a while after simply saying, "I get it now. I get God." They also turned their life around and pulled themselves out of the pit they were stuck in because someone showed them what was possible to reach with God.

> "Instead, be kind to each other, tender-hearted, forgiving one another, just as God through Christ has forgiven you" (Eph. 4:32).

Goodness

It's very hard to see and be the good in difficult trials, especially when all we feel is bad. Maybe you do not even realize how negative you have been during your depression. It's as common as someone asking you how you feel during the valley. Instead of responding "good," we choose negative responses to mirror what we feel. "How are you doing, any better?" Not so good, okay, bad, awful, depressed are just some responses I have gotten when asking someone's status during their wilderness. Of course, it's okay to be honest, but remember who is listening, your enemy. We don't want to make his job easier and dwell on his work. "I am still having some hard days still, but I am getting better!"

> "But you are not like that, for you are a chosen people. You are royal priests, a holy nation, and God's very own possession. As a result, you can show others the goodness of God, for he called you out of the darkness into his wonderful light" (1 Pet. 2:9).

> "So we keep on praying for you, asking our God to enable you to live a life worthy of his call. May he give you the power to accomplish all the good things your faith prompts you to do" (2 Thess. 1:11).

Faithfulness

In uncertain times, Satan's favorite tool is doubt, which can deplete your faith immensely. I have encountered many people in their trials comment on their faith and how it is endangered. Sometimes we don't know who to point the finger at, leaving God as a false culprit. "How could He let this happen? I thought He loved us?" This has Israelites written all over it. They doubted God in the midst of his work, and He was very clear on His covenant with them. By doubting and canceling out their faith, they were unable to reach their breakthrough sooner where they were to enjoy the land God blessed them with.

> "The Lord rewards everyone for their righteousness and faithfulness" (1 Sam. 26:23).

Gentleness

When it comes to anxiety and depression, everyone handles it in different ways as we all have our own unique personalities. Some of us are reserved, quiet, and just soak in our scary thoughts in torment. I know I didn't like getting upset with my family because I was afraid they wouldn't want to be around me anymore. Others may be harsh and have anger that they take out on people they love. I have heard the phrase before, "Hurting people hurt people." Now again, not everyone's personality during depression matches this, but it is something to try to monitor.

"Let your gentleness be evident to all"
(Phil. 4:5).

Self-Control

Remember my biggest fear was "losing my mind"? I definitely had an issue with self-control, not physically but mentally. Think of your goal in getting out of depression. It is to break the chains of control Satan has tormented you with.

"Like a city whose walls are broken through
is a person who lacks self-control" (Prov. 25:28).

How can we remain in our fortress if we are allowing the walls to be broken due to our poor self-control? We need to be in a fortified place that is centered on stability, which only God can provide. Allowing fear, anxiety, obsessive scary thoughts to take up residence in our mind is a sign of lacking self-control. I do not want you to feel badly about this. I've been there too! God gives us free will in life, the ability to make our decisions here on earth. Therefore, we are to remain stable in our swarming temptations by maintaining our self-control. An example of being on top of self-control is casting our care when anxiety strikes. We have talked about this a while back, but that mind-set takes a lot of control to accomplish! We are talking about something that has tormented you to the point of causing physical and mental attacks for who knows how long and giving it over to God. That isn't always easy to do, but with God, all things are possible.

> So then, let us not be like the others, who are asleep, but let us be alert and self-controlled. For those who sleep, sleep at night, and those who get drunk, get drunk at night. But since we belong to the day, let us be self-controlled, putting on faith and love as a breastplate, and the hope of salvation as a helmet. For God did not appoint us to suffer wrath but to receive salvation through our Lord Jesus Christ. He died for us so that, whether we are awake or asleep, we may live together with him. Therefore encourage one another and build each other up, just as in fact you are doing.(1 Thess. 5:6–11)

I won't dig much deeper as I need to begin closing, but it is up to you to study, pray, and dwell on these attributes. If any of them need maintenance, there are plenty of resources to aid you in this. Go to God, read your Bible, look into books, articles, Bible studies, or just ask a friend godly advice on how they overcame their struggle. In order to lower my anger and increase my patience with my children, I read about patience in the Bible, studied ways to keep peace in disciplining my kids, and asked friends for godly advice. Our contentment can't be controlled by our circumstances. We have a strong role in this, and God has you covered!

YOUR SEND OFF

I got this awesome visual of us in our pit when I started writing this book. Forgive me for my lack in artistic detail, but pretend you are in this huge hole in the ground and the sides are so steep that it is impossible to climb out. You look up and you can see the sky and these beautiful clouds floating by. There is a whole world out there, and you are missing it all while feeling lonely and scared. You are calling for help and reaching up for someone to grab you out of there. The thing is, we overlook this very important detail: *Jesus is in the pit with you.* There hasn't been one second that has passed that he wasn't there. Instead of pulling you out from above, He will stabilize you from underneath, allowing you to have enough strength to get your footing and climb out. You will get out. You are more than a conqueror.

> "He brought me out into a spacious place;
> he rescued me because he delighted in me" (2
> Sam. 22:20).

When I was at the rock bottom, I knew I had nothing to give back to God at that time. I was so broken. But I started seeing what would be beneficial from this experience, and I got sight of the other side. I could help other people get through this if I found the way and clung to God. I started praying, "God, if you just help me figure this out, I promise I will help anyone you bring to me." I would beg and beg and beg for him to help me through and the promise of using it for good was true in my heart. I know where I came from, and I am grateful that I made it out alive! Therefore, I will continue to serve God and help His children whenever needed. The amazing thing is, it's not something I have to force myself to do. I thrive in it. I have such a passion for this ministry. It brings me to life. So you can use that as your motivation. Your circumstances may be very different than mine. Everyone's story is unique.

Maybe you've been through abuse, loss, abandonment, divorce, financial hardship, etc. All these struggles are soaked with anxiety and depression and get people into pits. You can relate to those that are experiencing what you have, and they will physically see with their eyes a child of God that made it through. I feel honored that God chose this calling for me, and I love seeing people overcome what was once swallowing them. During your wilderness and trials, God is equipping you for your calling. You will not be the same person from here on out, and it's going to be okay. He is molding you into something you could not have been without your depression.

I hope this book has opened your eyes to many things and gives you the nudge you need to reach your breakthrough. I am so proud of you for striving to climb out of your pit and allowing God to help you. I pray that you get close with God and accept Him to enter into your situation fully! Please know that I understand you. I get it. It's always helpful to have at least one person to relate to. I'll be that for you! My healing really gained ground when others would tell me, "Yes! That's how I felt!" I love just simply telling people I coach, "I understand, I have been in that dark place." You were made for a purpose in this world, and somehow God is using this valley to bring you to a mountain for a reason! I believe in my heart that He leaves nothing unnoticed, not one thing is a mistake. He knew before your situation approached, and He sought you specifically for this battle. I find it to be an honor when God allows us to go through something, because He knows we have the strength to make it through with Him by our side.

I am going to close with a word of prayer, and please know I will continue to pray for you. You are not alone in your pain and struggle. You've got God and none of it is a surprise to him. Fight on, warrior!

Dear Jesus, thank you so much for bringing this child of yours alongside me in my chance at reaching them in their pain. They are worn and ready to thrive and live life in the moment, surrounded by the blessings you give them. Please let them hear your beautifully guided voice and show them the way out of their pit. Thank you so much for our valleys that we overcome and allowing us to build our strength and endurance through you. In Jesus's name, I pray, amen.

"We have this hope as an anchor for the soul, firm and secure. It enters the inner sanctuary behind the curtain, where our forerunner, Jesus, has entered on our behalf" (Heb. 6:19–20).

ABOUT THE AUTHOR

Hannah is a graduate of Rochester College and currently a stay-at-home mom of two. Her favorite activities include family outings, writing, and hunting for sea glass on the beaches of Virginia. While struggling with anxiety and depression, God showed her the way out, and she thrives in helping others do the same.

CPSIA information can be obtained
at www.ICGtesting.com
Printed in the USA
BVHW081950151221
624018BV00005B/731